SAVED IN ETERNITY

SAVED IN ETERNITY
THE ASSURANCE OF OUR SALVATION

Martyn Lloyd-Jones

Edited by Christopher Catherwood

CROSSWAY BOOKS • WHEATON, ILLINOIS
A DIVISION OF GOOD NEWS PUBLISHERS

First printing, 1988

Third printing, 1991

Printed in the United States of America

Library of Congress Catalog Card Number 87-71901

ISBN 0-89107-448-1

All Biblical quotations are taken from
the *King James Version.*

Contents

Preface

1. The Lord's Own Prayer   9
2. Why Pray?   23
3. The Glory of God in the Plan of Salvation   39
4. Our Security in God   53
5. The Lord Jesus Christ, the Lord of Glory   67
6. Antidote to Introspection   81
7. It Is Finished   95
8. The Hour Is Come   107
9. 'That He Should Give Eternal Life to
   as Many as Thou Hast Given Him'   121
10. The Only True God   135
11. A New Principle   147
12. Filled with Life Anew   159
13. Safe in His Eternal Kingdom   173

Preface

The sermons in this book form the first part of a series on John 17 which Dr Lloyd-Jones delivered on Sunday mornings in Westminster Chapel between 1952 and 1953. (Subsequent volumes will be published over the next few years.) These particular sermons were preached between April and July 1952, a period when Dr James Packer felt that he was 'on a plateau of supreme excellence'. Many others would endorse that view today, which is why these sermons have now been published.

CHRISTOPHER CATHERWOOD
Editor

I

The Lord's Own Prayer

John 17:1

It is customary for us to refer to the prayer which we find recorded in the Sermon on the Mount and in Luke 11 as the Lord's Prayer; but in reality, of course, that was the prayer which he gave as a kind of model to his disciples and to others, whereas here we have what can truly be called our Lord's own prayer, for here we find him praying his own personal prayer to the Father. The circumstances in which he came to do so are familiar to all of us. 'These words spake Jesus', are a reference to the great and mighty discourse which is recorded in chapters 14, 15 and 16 of this gospel. Then, having spoken those words about the Holy Spirit who is to be given to the believers, about what he could do in them, and all the results of his coming, our Lord lifted up his eyes to heaven and began to pray.

A quaint preacher in the seventeenth century said what is, I believe, the eternal truth about this prayer: 'It is the greatest prayer that was ever offered on earth and it followed the greatest sermon that was ever preached on earth'. In a sense nothing can be added to that. Here you have this sermon in those three chapters, then, immediately at the close of the sermon, our Lord offers up this prayer. It is one of the richest and most sublime statements to be found anywhere, even in the Scriptures themselves. And there is a sense in which one

9

preaches it with fear and trembling, lest one may in any way detract from its greatness and from its value. There have been those in the past who have felt that here we are dealing with something which is so sacred, because it is the very opening into our Lord's own heart, that the only right thing to do with this prayer is to read it. There was a great man living in Germany in the seventeenth century called Stein (the leader in many ways of the great Pietist Movement which was practised by the Moravian Brethren and others) who said he dared not preach on John 17, and there have been many others who have agreed with him.

Yet it seems to me that that is a mistake, for I would argue that our Lord would never have uttered this prayer audibly unless he had intended that we should hear it and that we should be able to study it and, above all, that we should be able to grasp its teaching. He did not merely pray to God, he prayed *audibly* to God, and the disciples heard him. Thus the prayer was preserved, and it seems to me that in this we have a wonderful illustration of the kindness of our Lord in allowing his disciples to hear this prayer and in arranging that it should be recorded in this way.

And, of course, as you look through the history of the church you will find that this prayer has been used of the Spirit in a very exceptional way to sustain people and to support them as they face difficulties in life, and especially when their time has come to die. The most notable example, perhaps, is that of John Knox, that great leader in the Protestant Reformation in Scotland, and mighty man of God. It is said that during the last days of his life, realizing that he was about to die, he asked his wife to read John 17 to him, and it was actually as she was reading this wonderful chapter that he passed from time to eternity. This is in no way surprising when you come to realize the wealth that there is here for us.

I am calling attention to it now because I am more and more convinced that half our troubles are due to the fact that

THE LORD'S OWN PRAYER

we fail to realize what exactly is offered in the Scriptures. All our anxieties and troubles, all our uncertainties and hesitations, and so much of our unhappiness in our spiritual lives, is to be traced simply to the fact that we do not realize what is provided for us. The apostle Peter, in his second epistle, does not hesitate to say that 'all things that pertain to life and godliness' are given to us (2 Pet 1:3). And the claim that is made constantly in these New Testament epistles is that there is no conceivable condition which we can ever know, there is no state of the soul which we can ever enter on, that has not already been prepared for. There is teaching concerning it, and God's people are meant to be people who are always rejoicing in the Lord. We are meant to know the fullness and the triumph, we are meant to experience a glory even here on earth.

But the question that arises is this: why are we not all, therefore, glorying and rejoicing in this great salvation? Why is it that so often we are apologetic and give the impression of being defeated? Why are we often so fearful of the world and of the future, concerned about God's cause and about the church? Why do we frequently, in this morbid concern, resort frantically to things that are often unworthy? Now I suggest that the explanation of all these things is our failure to realize what is provided for us, our failure, if you prefer it, to realize our position in Christ, and to enter into our heritage. We are, of course, entirely without excuse because, as I have been reminding you, it is all here for us. If we had nothing but John 17 we would surely have more than enough to sustain us, because here our Lord has given us an insight into our whole position, and into everything that is of importance and of value to us while we are in this world of time. We can do nothing better, therefore, than to look at this prayer, and to consider what he has to say.

Here is the position. He was about to leave the disciples, he knew how troubled they were, because they had already shown it, and he had started his sermon by saying, 'Let not

your heart be troubled.' They were troubled because he had
just been telling them that he was about to go from them,
and that had come as a shattering piece of information. Here
they were, they had been following him for three years, they
had listened to his teaching, they had observed his miracles,
they had come to rely upon him, and he had given them
certain powers. If there was a problem or difficulty they
turned to him at once and put their questions; he was always
ready to answer, and he was very patient. And now, after
these wonderful three years and after all this intimacy and
rich fellowship, he tells them that he is about to leave them.
They are utterly crestfallen and dumbfounded, and he, looking at them, can see it. He reads their minds and understands
their spirits, and so he begins by saying, 'Let not your heart
be troubled, ye believe in God, believe also in me.' Then he
proceeds to unfold for them this wonderful doctrine, this, to
them, amazing idea that it was expedient for them that he
should go away, that they were going to be in a better, not a
worse, position as a result of his going, because he was going
to prepare a place for them. Not only that, he was going to
send them another Comforter who would be *in* them and he
would come and dwell in them by the Holy Spirit—that
extraordinary doctrine of the indwelling Christ, of the abid-
ing of the Father and the Son in the very life of the believer.
And he goes on to work out and explain that blessed and
wonderful doctrine.

But he does not stop at that. He now prays for them, in
order that they may know that when he has left them here on
earth, when he has gone to be with the Father, he is still
going to go on praying for them. He says in verse 11, 'And
now, I am no more in the world, but these are in the world
and I come to thee. Holy Father, keep through thine own
name those whom thou hast given me . . .' He not only tells
them in doctrine and teaching, he wants them here to see that
he is committing them to the Father, so that they may know
that they are never left to themselves, but that in all circum-

√ stances and conditions he will still be looking after them. He will be their great Intercessor, indeed the Father himself is concerned about them. That is his object and purpose in praying this prayer audibly, that they may come to know, while he is still with them, the concern that he has about them, and will continue to have even though he is going to be out of their sight.

That is the essence of this prayer and what I want to do now is to take a general view of the prayer. Later I hope to consider it more in detail, and to expound and unfold its rich, its glorious and priceless teaching. Let me ask some questions before we go any further. How often have you read this chapter? What has been the value of this chapter to you hitherto? How often have you explored its riches? How often have you turned to it in distress? Do you understand John Knox's feeling when he wanted it to be read to him? It does seem to me that many of us are guilty of putting this great prayer as it were on one side in a kind of mock humility. Our greatest danger—indeed I feel it is my greatest danger—is to read the Scriptures too generally instead of looking into them, listening to every phrase, taking hold of every utterance, asking questions concerning every statement. Every one of these statements has a profound and rich meaning if we but take the trouble to look for them.

Let us, then, begin to do that together. Let us take a general view of this prayer, and discover some of the obvious lessons which are here on the very surface. The first thing which I think we must learn is how to pray. It is, after all, a model prayer, not in the sense that the so called Lord's
√ Prayer is a model prayer, but in the sense that this is the way in which our Lord himself prayed, and it is an example, or an illustration in practice. We can always be quite certain that the right way to pray is the way in which he prayed. His whole life, in a sense, was a life of prayer. Though he was the Son of God, he spent so much of his time praying, and this is his way of praying.

Now we all need instruction on this matter. We sometimes think that prayer is simple, but it is not. The great saints of all the centuries are agreed in saying that one of the most difficult things of all is to learn how to pray. If any Christian has been feeling cast down because he or she has found prayer difficult, they must not be discouraged, because it is the common experience of the saints. The person I am worried about is the one who has no difficulty about prayer, there is certainly something wrong about him. Prayer is the highest achievement of the saint. It does not just mean 'saying a prayer'—incidentally, what a horrible phrase that is—people talk about 'saying a prayer', but that is a very different thing from praying. It is a comparatively easy thing to say or read a prayer, but the main thing is to pray, and here we find our Lord praying.

You will see that there is a great logical sequence in the various petitions; our Lord does not merely utter a number of petitions at random, there is a definite arrangement, there is a very precise order, so that we have to realize that in prayer we must exercise a certain amount of discipline. The first thing always in prayer is to recollect ourselves—the act of recollection—a pausing to meditate and consider what exactly we are about to do. We begin to realize the Person whom we are going to address, and that leads to a certain inevitable consequence which will emerge as we analyse this great prayer.

John 17, therefore, is a wonderful illustration of the way in which we should pray. But at the same time it at once leads us into an understanding of who this person is who begins to pray. There is no chapter, perhaps, which gives us a greater insight into the person of our blessed Lord himself than this very prayer which we are considering together. He addresses his Father: 'Glorify thy Son, that thy Son also may glorify thee'; he talks about the glory which he had with the Father before the foundation of the world. We are at once reminded that we are in the presence of no mere man, we are in the

presence of the Son of God—the God-Man—the One who
shared the glory of the Father before the foundation of the
world, from all eternity, and as we go on with our consideration of this prayer we shall be led into some of the richest
and profoundest doctrines concerning the person and the
work of our Lord and Saviour Jesus Christ.

Now I have often emphasized the point that there is nothing which is so marvellous about Scripture as the way in
which it varies its presentation of the truth. There is a great
objective, dogmatic pronouncement of the truth concerning
the person and work of the Lord Jesus Christ, but sometimes
you will find that doctrine most perfectly taught in illustration and in practice, in the things which he says about
himself, or in the things which he assumes, and as we consider this prayer we come face to face with this rich doctrine
concerning this blessed person. Oh, if we could but lay a
firm hold upon it and realize again that the Son of God came
down into this world of time—we are facing here the whole
mystery and glory of the incarnation, of the virgin birth, the
humiliation of the Son of God. But the astounding thing is
that this person who is praying to the Father, was equal to
the Father. He assumed human nature, he came in the flesh,
he lived as man in the likeness of sinful flesh, and here he is
himself praying. Indeed, we read elsewhere of him crying
out, with strong crying and tears, unto his Father. It is a
marvellous, wonderful thing to contemplate, that God has
come down in the flesh in order to rescue and redeem us, and
opens his heart here to show us his wonderful concern for us,
and his amazing love with respect to us; and as we go on we
shall enter into this rich doctrine concerning his person.

And in a very specific manner we find here, in his approach, the whole reason why he came into the world. He
tells us that he had a certain task laid upon him, he came
to do it, and, still more glorious, he has done it. But as we
listen to him praying, we have, if we have never seen it
before, an insight into his reason for doing it—we begin to

see the plan of salvation. Now here again is something which
we modern Christians have ceased to remember, and what a
loss it is to us. Our fathers, in the great days of evangelism,
used to speak about the 'plan of salvation', 'the scheme of salvation'. We hear very little about that today. We are so
subjective, we are so interested in particular benefits, far too
infrequently do we stand back and view the whole grand
sweep of the plan of salvation. But you find it all here, you
will find it as he speaks of that glory in eternity before the
foundation of the world. You will see him leading us on step
by step and then going back into that glory. You cannot
listen to this prayer, or read it, without starting in glory and
without ending in glory, and without, in the meantime, having come right down to the very depths of the degradation
and shame of the cross and then to the rising again. It is all
here: the great plan with regard to us; this great purpose of
God with respect to certain people whom he has given to his
Son as the special object of salvation, and all that is to be
done for them in order to bring them to that ultimate consummation.

I know nothing which is more encouraging and more
exhilarating than that. There is no greater ground of security
in this world of time than to feel that you are a part of the
grand plan and purpose of God. None of these things are
accidental, none of them are fortuitous. It does not matter
what may happen in the future, nothing can disturb this
plan. My friend, if you are a Christian, do you know that
you were the object of God's interest and concern before the
foundation of the world? All these things have been worked
out in eternity, before time, so we must always remember
that nothing can happen in time which will make the
slightest difference. That is the argument which we find so
constantly in the Scriptures. We must never be tired of quot-
ing those great words: 'For I am persuaded, that neither
death, nor life, nor angels, nor principalities, nor powers,
nor things present, nor things to come, nor height, nor

depth, nor any other creature, shall be able to separate us from the love of God, which is in Christ Jesus our Lord' (Rom 8: 38-39). And if you have ever been in any doubt about that, read this prayer and see the security as he outlines it here.

And then we come on to look at what he has done for us. 'I have finished the work which thou gavest me to do,' he says, and as we go on from that we see that he has done certain things for us which none other could ever do for us and which we can never do for ourselves. He has been telling his disciples about it in the earlier chapters, and here he sums it up. What he has done for us is that he has satisfied the law and all its demands. It is amazing to me how people can look at and preach about Christ, his life and death and never mention the law. But unless the law of God is satisfied, there is no salvation. The law is opposed to us; it stands there and demands a perfect, absolute obedience and it threatens us with death if we fail in any one respect. If Christ has not fulfilled the law, we are yet in our sins, we are undone, we are damned and we are lost; but he has finished the work, the books have been cleared, the law has been satisfied, there is therefore no condemnation to them that are in Christ Jesus. Do you know that? Are you rejoicing in it? Are you ready to take your stand with Toplady and say:

> The terrors of law and of God
> With me can have nothing to do,
> My Saviour's obedience and blood
> Hide all my transgressions from view.

What a wonderful thing it is that here, just before he actually goes to the cross, he anticipates it all. He knows what he is going to do, and there is no uncertainty about it. He says, 'I have finished the work which thou gavest me to do.' It is already done, it is complete. We preach, therefore, a completed salvation. There is nothing left for us to do but to receive it; there is nothing that we must add to it; there is no

good work or any merit that we must provide: it is all in
Christ and in Christ alone. And we have a wonderful view
of that as we go through this prayer.

The next thing, therefore, is a realization of some of the
things that are possible for us even in this world and life. I
would remind you again that because of this blessed doctrine
we should be rejoicing. All the fruits of the Spirit should be
manifest in our lives—a joy and peace, longsuffering, gentleness, goodness, meekness, temperance and faith, all these
things should be present possessions. The Christian man,
according to this doctrine, is not hoping to be saved, he is
not constantly dwelling in mysteries, sometimes better,
sometimes worse; no, he is a man who rejoices in Christ
Jesus—listen to Paul: 'Rejoice in the Lord always: and again I
say, rejoice' (Phil 4:4). But are we rejoicing? Do we realize
the possibility of rejoicing? If we only grasp what this prayer
is saying, and understand this teaching, we shall be able to
smile in the face of the world and in the face of hell. He
means us to be rejoicing, to know this fullness that God has
provided for us in him, and, I say, shame on us, Christian
brothers and sisters, unless we are partaking of it, partici-
pating in it, and rejoicing in it altogether!

Here, in his prayer, the Lord allows us to see something of
this wonderful possibility, and then, as I have already hinted,
he shows us the source of security and strength in this world.
Can you imagine anything that is more comforting than this,
that the Lord Jesus Christ has prayed for you: 'Neither pray I
for these alone, but for them also which shall believe on me
through their word'? Do you realize that when he was praying this prayer the Lord Jesus Christ was praying for *you*?
Now, if we are Christians, we all like to have people praying
for us. There are many people in the Christian life today
because somebody prayed for them, a saintly father or
mother, perhaps, who prayed throughout the years of dis-
appointment, and went on praying. And God heard the
prayer and they have become Christians. Is there anything

that gives greater consolation than to know that people are
praying for you? I know of nothing that is a greater encouragement to me, in my work and in my ministry, than to
know that people are praying for me. They are going to God
who is the source of all power and asking him to fill me with
power.

So, then, if you believe in the prayer of a saintly person,
how much more should you believe in the prayer of the Son
of God for you. Here he lets us know that he prayed for us
and he goes on praying for us, and, most wonderful of all,
what he does is to put us into the hands of God. He says:
'Holy Father, keep through thine own name those whom
thou hast given me, that they may be one, as we are. While I
was with them in the world, I kept them in thy name: those
that thou gavest me I have kept . . . and now come I to thee'
(verses 11-13). 'Father,' he says in effect, 'I hand them back
to you, you keep them.' If only we could somehow take
hold of this wonderful truth, that the Lord Jesus Christ,
himself, has put us into the safe keeping of God and that we
are therefore in God's safe keeping! Our Lord was never
tired of expounding this doctrine. In the Sermon on the
Mount, for instance, what he keeps on saying, in effect, is,
'Foolish people, if only you realized that God is your Father,
if only you realized his concern for you, if only you took to
heart the lesson of the birds and the flowers! Look at his
concern for them—how much greater is his concern about
you, oh you of little faith.' And here, in his last prayer, he
hands us over to the Father's care and says, 'Father, keep
them.' Oh, it is a wonderfully consoling and comforting
thought, to know that God the Father is looking upon us,
and caring for us, and keeping us at this present time.

And finally we are going to learn from this prayer what is
our relationship to this world, and our business in it. We
have not only been saved for our own sakes, we have been
saved in order that we may pass on this good news to others.
'As thou hast sent me into the world, even so have I also sent

them'—he was leaving them in the world with a message, he was sending them to do something, as God had sent him before.

So there we have hurriedly looked at some of the things that stand out on the very surface of this prayer. You will find there are certain natural divisions: from verses 1–5 our Lord prays mostly for himself and about himself; then from verses 6–19 he prays for the disciples in particular, those who are around and about him; and from verses 20–26 he prays for the church universal at all times and in all places. There is the logical division to which I have just referred. He starts with adoration and worship, his prayer for himself, then prays for the disciples and then for those who are going to believe through the demonstration of the disciples. In other words, it is a great prayer that covers the whole of the Christian era and the entire course of the Christian church. Therefore, as we study it, we must observe it very carefully, and especially the way our Lord approaches his Father.

There are certain things about which we should always be certain, things about which Christ was certain. First: 'Father,' he says. He is not in doubt about him. He addresses God as Father six times—he knows the relationship, he was one with the Father from all eternity. God is his Father in the sense that he is the Father in the blessed Trinity of Father, Son and Holy Ghost. God is also his Father in the sense that Jesus has now become man and so is looking to God as his Father. Again, God is now his Father because he, the Son, is the representative of the many brethren whom he has come to save and for whom he has come to die. As he is the first born of many, many brethren, so God is his Father in that sense, in the relationship of the children to God their heavenly Father.

But notice that he not only addresses him as 'Father'. In verse 11 he addresses him as 'holy Father'. How vital it is to remember that—that God is holy. He is our Father who is in heaven, so his name must be hallowed. We must always approach him with reverence and godly fear for our God is a consuming fire. Though our Lord was one with the Father, though nothing had ever come between them, though he never needed to ask for forgiveness of his own sins because he had never sinned, he still addressed God as holy Father. How often do we forget that even our blessed Lord addressed him as holy Father?

Lastly, he addresses him as 'righteous Father'—'O righteous Father,' he says in verse 25, 'the world hath not known thee: but I have known thee, and these have known that thou hast sent me.' This is a wonderful thought and when he says this, he is referring to the character of God, to the faithfulness of God. In other words, our Lord is saying, in effect, 'I know that what you have promised, you will perform. You have made certain promises to me concerning these people for whom I have done this work, and I know that you will never fail in any one respect with regard to all those promises. You are a righteous Father.'

If we remember nothing else from this study, God grant that we should learn just that, that when we pray in Jesus Christ's name, we are praying to *our Father*. Yes, he is the great, almighty, eternal God, but he has become our Father in Christ. He is a holy Father, nothing unworthy must be mentioned in his presence; we must not present unworthy desires, nor selfish thoughts before our holy Father. But, thank God, he is a righteous Father, faithful and just, and if we truly confess he forgives us all our sins and cleanses us from all unrighteousness. As you come before him, conscious of your sins and maybe doubtful and hesitant, remember this, he is righteous, he has promised forgiveness in Christ. Remember his righteousness and remember that every promise that he has ever given, he will most certainly and most surely fulfil.

Oh, how we should thank God that our Lord offered this prayer audibly, and how we should thank God that it has been recorded! Let us look into these things. Let us meditate upon them. I know of no wealthier place than this. Let us enter into it. Let us receive of these riches, that we may realize that while we live in this world of time there are certain things that are absolutes surrounding and encompassing us, and that we are in the hands of One who has said, 'I will never leave thee, nor forsake thee' (Heb 13:5).

2

Why Pray?

John 17:1

I should like to look once more at John 17 in a more or less
general sense, not so much from the standpoint from which
we have just seen it, but rather as this chapter and this prayer
have some lessons to teach us about the whole subject of
prayer itself. I sometimes think that there is no subject, perhaps, in connection with the Christian life, which causes so
many people such perplexity as this one, I think we all
understand very well the feelings of the disciples when they
turned to our Lord on one occasion and said, 'Lord, teach us
to pray,' because, for some peculiar reason, prayer does tend
to be a problem to people. I think any pastor of souls will
agree with me when I say that this question of prayer is one
that is very frequently brought to his notice. Anyone who
takes the Christian life at all seriously is probably concerned
about his or her prayer life, and very great difficulties and
perplexities often surround this question.

Now obviously in the space of one sermon I cannot hope
to deal with all the problems, indeed, I am not proposing to
go into it in detail—that would require a whole series of
sermons on the subject of prayer as such. I am simply concerned to gather certain general lessons which seem to me at
any rate to be taught us on the very surface of the prayer of
our Lord which is recorded in this particular chapter. In

order to concentrate attention on this, let me put it to you in this form. I think there are two main difficulties that tend to present themselves to people as they contemplate this whole question of prayer, and these perplexities are generally due to two extreme positions which have been taken up by Christian people in the past and are still taken up by some today.

First of all there is the extreme position of those who seem to have no difficulty in prayer, the people who give the impression that there is nothing so easy or so simple. They are very fond of using the phrase 'prayer changes things', and give us the impression that whatever their problem, the answer comes and all is well. They are sure that nobody should be in trouble about these matters, that prayer is the most natural thing in the world, involving no effort, no difficulty at all; they just do it so easily and talk so glibly about it.

That, I think, is a position which does raise problems and queries in the minds of many other Christian people, who find it very difficult to reconcile that with some of the plain teaching of Scripture. Those friends who find prayer so easy seem to forget all the conditions that are attached to these promises and to these great offers. There are many souls who, having listened to such teaching and having tried honestly and genuinely to put it into practice, have found that it does not work out like that with them. As a consequence, being disappointed, they begin to question the goodness of God. They question all the teaching of the Scriptures with regard to the Fatherhood of God and with regard to the whole question of prayer. This perplexity arises from exaggerations on the part of that particular school which I have just described.

But, on the other hand, there is another position which is taken up by some and which again leads to all sorts of difficulties and perplexities. It is the position of those who more or less deny the value and the point of prayer at all. Their

argument is that God knows everything and that everything
that happens, happens as the result of God's will, and therefore, surely, there is no point in praying. God is omniscient,
they say. He knows everything; he is the sovereign Lord of
the universe; nothing does happen or can happen outside his
will or control. And so they question the purpose of prayer.
This is the position which is sometimes described as deter-
minism. It is an attitude which regards life and everything
that happens in this world as being part of a rigid and closed
process, and clearly, if that is true, there is no point in prayer.
Furthermore, there are many people who have so exag-
gerated the doctrine of the sovereignty of God, or have
drawn such wrong deductions from it, that they have ren-
dered those who listen to their arguments and teaching almost incapable of praying with any sense of confidence and
assurance.

There, then, are the main positions. I have chosen these
two simply because they are the two extremes, but many
others are to be found between them. The question, therefore, arises as to how we approach all this. How do we try to
arrive at the true position with regard to prayer, in the light
of these two extreme positions that lead us to so many
problems and perplexities? Well, I would lay it down as a
principle at this point—and it is applicable not only to this
question of prayer but to many other problems as well—that
the one thing we have to do in a situation like this is to avoid
becoming slaves to our own theories and ideas and to our
own understanding of the truth. In avoiding that danger we
should go to the Scriptures, and look at the Bible's plain and
obvious teaching with as dispassionate and open a mind as
we are capable of. We should do that, I say, not only with
regard to this problem of prayer, but with regard to any
other problem that may arise in our spiritual experience.
There are certain doctrines taught in Scripture quite clearly,
but then we come up against something that we cannot quite
fit into our doctrinal pattern, and the danger at that point is

to stand on our own doctrine and to try to explain away the Scripture. If ever we find a point that seems to conflict with our clear grasp of doctrine, it seems to me that, for the time being, the essence of wisdom is to leave our doctrine where it is. It is not that we deny it, we just leave it for the moment, we come back to Scripture and we note what Scripture has to say everywhere about this particular matter. Then having done that, we again attempt to relate this obvious and clear teaching of Scripture with the doctrine of which we are equally sure.

Now that is the kind of thing which we must do with this whole question of prayer, and fortunately there is a great wealth of material in the Bible at our disposal. I am merely going to select certain points of which we can be absolutely sure, things which are beyond doubt and peradventure. I do not pretend I can solve every problem with regard to prayer; there are certain ultimate difficulties here, as there are with many other points touching our relationship to God, which perhaps we will never fully understand in this life and world. But it is our bounden duty to go as far as we can and to understand the teaching as far as that is possible.

The first obvious point is that a very prominent place is given in the Scriptures to prayer. According to Scripture, prayer is an important and essential element in the godly life. Indeed, the Scriptures actively teach us to pray, both by precept, and by example. We are exhorted to pray, our Lord himself exhorted people to do so. He said that men should always pray and not faint. He taught his disciples how to pray, and he urged them not to give up. You also find the same thing in the epistles: 'Keep steadfast in prayer' is their argument, always encouraging us to pray. Now whatever your view may be of the sovereignty of God and of man's relationship to him, you have to reckon with this obvious, plain teaching of the Scriptures, so that prayer must be a very prominent part of the life of any godly person in this world.

Furthermore, it is not only by precept that we are taught

to pray. We are taught by example also. If you read the Old Testament you will find that the patriarchs talked with God and spoke to him—that is prayer. Look at the psalms, most of them are prayers. Consider, for instance, Psalm 74; that is typical of the psalmists and of how these men prayed to God. Then you find prayers in the prophetic books, indeed you have them everywhere in the Old Testament. You also find the apostles praying, but above all, as we see in this great chapter, our Lord himself prayed, and all these facts urge us to pray. We see, then, that the Bible teaches us to pray, it urges us to pray, in a sense it pleads with us to pray.

But I can draw a second deduction, which is also very plainly taught in the Scriptures: the more saintly, the more godly a person, the more time he spends in prayer. Take any example you like in the Scriptures and you will find it absolutely invariable. Now if you and I had argued on general principles, we might have come to the opposite conclusion. We might have considered a man very saintly because his will was conforming to the will of God, and because he meditated about these things and because his supreme desire was to live to the glory of God. Well, you might say, such a man would have much less need of prayer than anybody else, but it is not the case. Look at the most outstanding godly men and women, how often they spent much more time in prayer than anybody else. They did not just passively wait for God's will to be done, no, they, more than anybody else, went, rather, and talked to God. And as you proceed to read the history of the church throughout the centuries, you will find exactly the same thing. Whether he belongs to the Roman Catholic Church or the Protestant Church, it is always the hallmark of a saint that he is a great man of prayer. John Wesley used to say that he had a very poor opinion of a Christian who did not spend at least four hours in prayer every day, and that is but a typical statement of God's outstanding people in the church throughout the centuries.

But, and this of course brings us directly to John 17, the

most striking and important thing of all is the fact that prayer
played such a prominent part in the life or our Lord himself.
Now I wonder whether we have ever stopped to contemplate that? Of course we all know that he prayed. We say
that we have read our gospels and have known that since we
were children. But I am not talking about an intellectual
awareness of the fact, I am asking whether we have ever
understood that fact, and meditated upon it, because the
more you stop to think about it, the more you see that one of
the most astounding things in Scripture is the fact that the
Lord Jesus Christ ever prayed at all. The fact is, however,
that he did pray, and not merely that he prayed, but that he
prayed constantly; indeed you find that he prayed for very
long periods. On one occasion he spent the whole night in
prayer—the Son of God praying right through the night! We
are constantly told that he rose a great while before dawn and
went up into a mountain somewhere to pray.

Now his disciples always noticed that he was praying, and
that was, in a sense, one of the things which prompted them
to ask him, 'Lord, teach us to pray.' They felt that he was
doing something which they did not quite understand; they
wondered what the reason was for the delight and pleasure
which he took in the act of prayer, and why it meant so
much to him. They could not say they felt like that. But they
knew that there was no one like him. They saw something in
his face and demeanour, they saw his miracles and they said,
Ah, there is something in that prayer life, oh that we might
have that!

They noticed especially the fact that he always prayed a
great deal, and in an exceptional way, in times of crisis and in
times of great importance. You remember it was before he
chose his twelve disciples that he spent the whole night in
prayer. This was a very important and a very vital decision
to take, so he spent the whole night in prayer to God before
he selected these men. There was another occasion when he
prayed like this, we read about it in John 6. He had just fed

the five thousand and some of the people were so deeply impressed that they decided that he was the Messiah, and that they must take him up to Jerusalem and crown him king. But when our Lord saw that they were going to take him by force and make him a king, he went up into a mountain, himself alone, and there he communed with God, and prayed to him. It was one of the critical moments in his life and experience. Here was a great temptation—he had already met it in the wilderness—to bring in his kingdom in a kind of human political sense, and the temptation was so strong that he went away alone to pray with God.

You find him doing it, too, at the grave of Lazarus. This again was a momentous, tremendous occasion—he was going to raise the dead—and so he prayed to God and thanked God that he knew that God had heard his voice and always heard it. Then you remember how he prayed just as he was going up to face the cross—you find it recorded in John 12:27-28—and, too, you see him praying in the Garden of Gethsemane, praying to the Father in an agony that produced blood-stained sweat. Then here we have this great high priestly prayer, in his last hours with his disciples before he goes to finish the work upon the cross, and here he prays audibly in their presence.

What, then, does all this teach us? We might very well spend much time in deducing certain things about the person of our Lord. We will not do that now, but at least we must note that it tells us a great deal about him. If ever you are in trouble about the incarnation this one prayer of our Lord's prayer life in general ought at once to put you at rest and keep you at rest. He is truly man. It is not a case of God in a kind of phantom body, it is not a theophany, it is the incarnation, the Word made flesh and dwelling among us. He is truly God, yes, but he is truly man. Here you begin to understand what Paul was talking about in Philippians 2, when he says, 'He emptied himself' (see the Revised Version). What Paul meant is that while he was here on earth

our Lord did not make use of his powers as God. And
because he lived as a man, prayer was essential to him—even
he could not go on without prayer. In other words, it teaches
us what he said so often himself, that he was entirely dependent upon his Father. He said, 'The words that I speak unto
you I speak not of myself: but the Father that dwelleth in me,
he doeth the works' (Jn 14:10).

That is the astounding thing about our Lord's life. Here he
is, very Son of God and perfect man, and yet he does nothing of himself, he gets all his orders, as it were, from God.
God gives him the words to speak, God tells him what to
do, and gives him the power to do it—that is why he prayed
before calling his disciples. He looked to God for light and
guidance, perfect man but in utter dependence upon his
Father. As God, there was no need for him to pray. As God,
he was co-equal with God, he was omniscient and all powerful, but here on earth we see him in his true character, the
mediator, God-Man. And as we watch him in prayer we see
him there as the appointed mediator, the One who has been
sent by God to do certain work and to complete it here on
earth for us. Therefore, to look at our Lord praying is perhaps one of the most wonderful doors of entry into the great
mystery of his blessed person. I repeat, if there is anyone in
trouble about the person of Christ, about the God-Man, oh,
just watch him praying, and you have to include that in your
doctrine of his person. So many think of him as God only,
with a kind of clothing of flesh. That is wrong, because if he
were God only, there would be no need for prayer. No, we
must insist upon man also—God-Man.

But next I want also to draw certain more general deductions about prayer itself, and I think we can draw them very
definitely from the points I have established. Watch those
patriarchs, watch King David, watch the prophets, all praying, and the more saintly they were the more they prayed.
Watch the apostles praying, and above all, watch the Son of
God praying. What, then, is prayer? What is the explanation

of all this? I suggest that we must inevitably come to the conclusion that prayer, to the Christian, to God's man, is something natural and almost instinctive; prayer is something which is expressive of the relationship between the child and the Father. Now I think that is a very important argument. You show me a man who does not pray very much and I will tell you the real problem of that man. It is that he does not know God, he does not know God as his Father. That is the trouble. The problem is not that he is not a moral man, or that he is not a good man. He can be highly moral, he may be very faithful in Christian church work, there may be nothing he is not prepared to do, but if he does not pray, I tell you that the essence of that man's trouble is that he does not know God as his Father. For those who know God best are the ones who speak to him most of all.

There is no need to prove a thing like this—the little child always speaks to his Father. Have you not often noticed how the child of some great man talks to him freely, while another man going into his presence is nervous. Not so the child; the child speaks freely, because he knows the relationship and so he speaks to his father. And that is why the most saintly people are the ones who pray most; that is why the Lord Jesus Christ prayed more than anybody else, because he knew God in a way nobody else knew him. That, then, is the way to approach this question of prayer. The whole trouble with people who get into difficulties over prayer is that they start at the end instead of at the beginning. You do not start with the desire for answers, you start with adoration, and it is because we forget this all important matter that we tend to get into such perplexities. To pray is the obvious, natural thing for a child to do and there is nothing that expresses more eloquently or more cogently the whole relationship of man to God as prayer. That is the first thing. So, then, I think that the saints and, supremely, our Lord himself, prayed to God, primarily, not to ask for things but to assure their own hearts and to maintain their contact with

God and to make certain of their contact and communion
with him.

Our whole idea of prayer is false. We think of prayer only
as guidance and requests. Now if you were to put that into
practice in human relationships you would regard it as insulting. No, the thing the saint wants to know above everything
else is that all is well between his soul and the Father. There is
nothing the saint delights in more than to know God as his
Father. He likes to maintain the contact and communion, to
assure his heart before God and in the presence of God. The
saint is in this difficult world, there are temptations from the
outside and the whole world is against us, and the saint is
tried—sometimes he almost despairs. So he goes to God
immediately, not to ask this or that but just to make certain
that all is well there, that the contact is unbroken and perfect,
that he can assure his heart and know that all is well.

That is what our Lord is doing here in John 17, and that is
the thing which stands out most frequently in this prayer.
Our Lord is assuring his own human heart in the presence of
his Father. We saw earlier how he did that when he was
raising Lazarus from the dead; indeed he puts it in words for
us: 'Then they took away the stone . . . And Jesus lifted up
his eyes, and said, 'Father'—he is praying—'I thank thee that
thou hast heard me'—always he is assured in his heart—'And
I knew that thou hearest me always: but because of the
people . . .' (Jn 11:41-42). He just turns to God. He knows
all is well, but, he is assuring his heart in the presence of God.

Let me put it like this: the saints always prayed to God,
and our Lord supremely did so, because they believed in
God's power, because they believed in God's ability to help,
and, above all, because they believed in God's willingness
and readiness to help. That is tremendously important.
They, of everybody, knew the power of God, yes, but the
world and its trials tend to shake our confidence in him and
there is no better way of reminding ourselves of the power
and the greatness of God, his ability and his readiness to help,

than to go and talk to him; that is why the saints always fly
to prayer. 'The name of the Lord is a strong tower: the
righteous runneth into it, and is safe' (Prov 18:10). In other
words, the saint rushes to God in prayer and reminds himself
of these things.

Prayer, in many ways, is the supreme expression of our
faith in God and our faith and confidence in the promises of
God. There is nothing that a man ever does which so proclaims his faith as when he gets down on his knees and looks
to God and talks to God. It is a tremendous confession of
faith. I mean by this that he is not just running with his
requests and petitions, but if he really waits upon God, if he
really looks to God, he is there saying, 'Yes, I believe it all, I
believe that you are a rewarder of them that diligently seek
you, I believe you are the Creator of all things and all things
are in your hands. I know there is nothing outside of your
control. I come to you because you are in all this and I find
peace and rest and quiet in your holy presence and I am
praying to you because you are what you are.' That is the
whole approach to prayer that you find in the teaching of
Scripture.

And finally I can put it in this way, that the saints and our
Lord clearly prayed to God in order that they might discover
his will. They were much more concerned about discovering
his will than having their own way and will. 'Ah,' they said,
'the one thing that matters at this juncture is that we may
know what God's will is', so they went into his presence. If
you read the marvellous prayers of the saints, as in Daniel 9,
for instance, you will learn a great deal about how to pray.
The prophet did not quite understand what God was doing.
The whole thing was perplexing to him and he went to God
and talked to God about it. He said various things to God of
which he was certain and then he said, in effect, 'I do not
quite understand this, but I want to do your gracious will
and you understand what you are doing.'

Jeremiah did exactly the same thing. God told him to go

and buy a particular field. Jeremiah's first reaction was that it
was impossible because God was also telling him that the
Children of Israel were going to be carried into captivity. If
this was going to happen, what was the point of buying a
field? Then he reminded himself of the great character of
God, and having done that he said, in effect, 'Enlighten my
perplexity, let me see what you are doing, explain your holy
will to me.'

We have now reached the point where we can draw certain general conclusions, and here they are. Whatever else I
do not understand about prayer, I think I now understand
this: that God has chosen to do his work in this world in that
way, through praying people. He need not have done so, he
could have done it without them, but it is perfectly clear that
God has ordained and decreed to do his work in this world
through men and women, like you and me, and through our
prayers. He calls us to pray. He urges us to do so and then he
answers our prayers—even though he could have done without our prayers at all.

'Ah,' says someone, 'that is what I want to know—why
does he do it?'

My dear friends, who can answer such a question? I cannot, but I thank God that he does it in that way. I do not
know why he elected to do it, but I know he does it. That is
his way and I accept it. And I am grateful for this reason: it is
in this way that God reveals himself to us. Read about prayer
in the Scriptures and especially watch these people praying,
even our Lord himself, and I think you will find that as the
result of prayer all these people come to know God better
than they would have ever known him apart from this. It is
in this way that God shows himself, and reveals his Father-
heart to us. For example, there is this difficult circumstance
with which I am faced. I do not know what to do. I tend to
become unhappy and miserable. But then I go to God and
wait upon him and he begins to show himself and his purpose to me; he reveals himself to me. If you have not learnt

more of God through prayer there is something wrong with your spiritual life. It is there that he teaches us things and in this way draws out our faith. So, then, since this is one of God's ways of revealing himself to mankind and bringing his purposes to pass, the whole problem and question of God's omnipotence is removed. You should never be perplexed by it. God has chosen to do these things in this way, so his omniscience should never arise as a problem. And in the same way I can say that it in no way affects the sovereignty of God. It is one of God's ways of displaying his sovereignty. There is no conflict between the sovereignty of God and prayer, for it is the sovereign God who has chosen to do his work in this world through praying men and women. Far from being contradictory, they work together.

And, finally, we can draw some wonderful practical conclusions from this teaching and especially from this chapter. The supreme object of prayer should be to glorify and magnify God and that is why we must always start by worshipping him. The model prayer does that: 'Our Father which art in heaven, Hallowed be thy name. Thy kingdom come . . .' Not, 'Give me this little request . . .' No, you start by worshipping. It is the personal relationship; you pray because you like the person, because you want to show your respect to the person, because you delight to be in the presence of the person—that is the essence of prayer.

Then another thing we can draw as a practical deduction— and I am grateful for it—is that God delights to be told things he knows already. I am addressing certain intellectuals who are very fond of making fun of people who in their prayers tell God certain things. You will have heard the criticism. But to tell God what he knows is an essential part of prayer. Read the Bible and you will find John, for example, telling God things he knew already. The writers of the psalms did the same thing—why? It is because God is a Father. God is not a machine, if I may say it with reverence. He is our Father, and as a Father he delights to be told these things by

his children. He means us to tell him, so do not be afraid to
tell God things he knows already. Do not say, 'God is omniscient and, because God knows everything, I must just
wait silently in his presence.' No, tell him these things, he
likes to hear, he wants to be in communion with you, he
delights in fellowship with you.

The next thing I would say is that our object in prayer
should never be to change God's heart or will. There is never
any need to do that, for if you think you need to change
God's heart you are insulting him. God's will is always perfect, and he is a loving Father. Rather, come to him to discover his will, to see that it is right and to rejoice in it—that is
the object of prayer. But that does not mean that you do not
take your requests to him. Again, as your Father, he is there
waiting for you to do that and willing for you to do that; he
is there ready to listen to our requests and petitions. So tell
him all about them. Do what these men did and what our
Lord did in the Garden of Gethsemane—'If it be possible . . .
nevertheless not as I will, but as thou wilt.' Make your requests known, tell him your desires but always immediately
say, 'I am so small and finite, I do not understand. This is
what I would like, but if it is not your will, well I do not ask,
I am content with your will, whatever it may be'—an attitude of utter resignation. If you have started your prayer
rightly, if you have started by glorifying God and saying,
'Hallowed be thy name, thy kingdom come on earth, thy
will be done,' and so on, you have already been saying,
'God, my supreme desire is that your will be done in me as
in the whole world.' Therefore you are very ready, when
you bring your requests, to say, 'If it be your will.' I cannot
understand the approach to prayer which says you should
not add 'If it be your will.' I have the authority of the Son of
God, the Lord Jesus Christ himself for saying that we must
always say, 'If it be your will.' It is *God's* will that has to be
done, so make your requests and desires known but always
submit utterly and absolutely to the will of God.

And the last point I make is this, that pleas and arguments and requests are perfectly legitimate in prayer. Have you noticed these men of God praying? They knew God was omniscient, yes, so they not only made their requests known to him but also pleaded with him. And what I like above everything else is the way they argued with him. Moses, for example, did so. On one occasion he came down from the Mount and found the people rebellious, and when he found God threatening to disown them and leave them to their own devices, Moses said to God, You cannot do this. Look too at the man in Psalm 74, who says, in effect, 'Lord why do you allow men to do these things?' I believe God as Father delights in listening to such pleas and reasonings and arguments. This flabby generation of Christians seems to have forgotten what our fathers used to delight in when they talked about 'pleading the promises'. They did not regard that as offensive. They had no sort of mock humility but they felt they were entitled, according to this teaching, to go to God as the psalmist did and remind him of his own promises. They said, 'Lord, I do not understand, I know it is my imperfection, but I am certain of these promises. Lord, help me to see how the promises are to be related to these perplexities.'

So it is perfectly right to plead with God; our Lord pleaded with him. In this great prayer he argued with God by bringing these requests. He reminded him of his own promises, and of his own character. I believe God delights in this as Father, and as we do these things in this way our hearts will be reassured before him and, oftentimes, we shall be amazed and astonished at the answers that we receive. Whatever happens, prayer will always bring us nearer and closer to God if we pray in the right and the true way.

So, then, we have looked together at this great prayer and at some of the great lessons that are obvious on the very surface; God grant that we may learn them and implement them. My dear friends, think before you pray. Go into the presence of God realizing that he is in heaven and that you are upon the earth. Look at these great examples, and above all look at your blessed Lord himself. Remember that he suffered against himself the contradiction of sinners, that he resisted unto blood striving against sin and that he prayed with cries of agony and with sweat and was heard because of his reverence and godly fear, though he was indeed the only begotten Son of God.

3

The Glory of God in the Plan of Salvation

John 17:1

So far, in considering this great prayer, we have been look-ing at the matter in general. We can now proceed to look at the actual subjects which our Lord dealt with in his prayer, the thoughts that were uppermost in his mind as thus he prayed to his heavenly Father. Let me remind you that the prayer can be divided into three main sections: the first is from verses 1–5, in which our Lord prays for himself; then in verses 5–19 we have his prayer for his immediate disciples, those who were around and about him; and from there on he prays for the church universal.

In the first section, where our Lord prays for himself, we find that the essence of his petition is that the Father may glorify him, in order that he also may glorify the Father: 'Father the hour is come; glorify thy Son, that thy Son also may glorify thee.' In other words, his main concern at this point is that he may glorify God. That is the supreme thing, but, you notice, he tells us why that is so, and he does this in terms of God's great purpose in the matter of our salvation. The whole idea here expressed is that our Lord is anxious that God's glory may be manifested, and manifested es-pecially in the salvation of men.

As a result, in these five verses we have one of the most marvellous displays of the whole gospel of salvation and of

39

the plan of salvation which is to be found anywhere in the
Scriptures. There is nothing which is more characteristic of
the Scriptures than the way in which here and there they give
us a kind of complete synopsis, or compendium, of doctrine
and theology. In this prayer in particular, our Lord opens
our eyes and instructs us with regard to some of the vitals
and fundamentals of our faith. And as one can well antici-
pate, in view of the fact that it is our Lord himself speaking
and praying, there is no more glorious statement of the
gospel than you find in these five verses.

Why is it, do you think, that we hear so little today about
the plan of salvation, the scheme, the whole object and purpose of it? I use the phrase that was so frequently used by our
fathers but which, for some reason, is so infrequently used
today. Our fathers delighted in looking at and contemplating, or, if I may use the words of Isaac Watts, *surveying*, the
plan of salvation. I have no hesitation in saying that most of
our troubles as Christian people, and the whole state of the
church today, is to be explained very largely by our failure to
consider the plan of salvation as a whole.

The trouble with us is, as I am never tired of pointing out,
that we are so utterly subjective. That is the essence of the
trouble with this modern generation to which you and I
belong. Now I am not talking about people outside the
church, but about ourselves, who are inside the church. It
may be that we have all been influenced by the climate of
thought and by this morbid interest in psychology and in
analysing ourselves, but whatever it is, we have become self-
centred and that is the curse of this generation. We are always looking at ourselves, at how things affect us and at
what we want for ourselves. Now there are many possible
explanations for that, which need not claim our attention
now, but the fact of the matter is that we are slaves to our
own habits and states and desires, and to our own likes and
dislikes, and the result is that we approach everything from
the standpoint of what it means to *us*. And the tragic thing is

THE GLORY OF GOD IN THE PLAN OF SALVATION 41

that we tend to approach the gospel of Jesus Christ in that particular way, with the result that we fail to realize the truth either about ourselves or about this wonderful salvation which we have, because we particularize on points. We look solely on what the gospel has to say 'to me', how the gospel can 'help me', and we fail, therefore, to hear what the gospel has to say about us, and we fail also to realize the scope and the greatness and the vastness of the gospel itself.

The writer of the epistle to the Hebrews described the gospel as 'so great a salvation'. My suggestion is that we seem to be missing this greatness at the present time and that this is simply because, instead of looking at it as it is, and as it is displayed here, we look at ourselves and what it has to give us. The gospel is presented purely in this personal manner and we forget the greatness which we discover when we look at God's plan of salvation as a whole, and when we allow the gospel to put it before our wondering gaze. You will find in many of our hymns that this idea of the greatness is most forcibly and magnificently expressed.

Charles Wesley says, "Tis mercy all, immense and free,' and yet so often the impression is given that the gospel is something subjective and small, something which just does this or that. Thank God it does these things, too, for me, but it is not only that. If you are subjective in your approach you will often find yourself feeling unhappy; if you think of the gospel as something coming to you, or happening in your life, immediately you will be upset and you will have nothing to fall back on. The tragedy of the subjective approach is that it is essentially so selfish that eventually it fails us.

But if we take this objective approach to start with and then come on to the subjective we shall gain everything; we shall start on such a vast plan and scheme that we shall be taken up into it, and when anything goes wrong with us, we will relate it to the whole. So to avoid that danger of the subjective, we must study the great subject which we have in these five verses. Not that we must study it for that reason only. It is our duty to study it and I want to impress that upon us all. We claim that we are so busy that we have not the time to read. We know our forefathers used to read the doctrines, but we have not got the time. We want it all in a nutshell, and we want to go through the whole gospel of John in one address. We want a bird's eye view of the whole Bible, and the result is that we miss the doctrine. But here it is displayed, and because God has displayed it to us here, it is our duty to study it, in order that we may find some of the great possibilities that lie open to us. It is a tragedy that we tend to live as paupers in the spiritual realm, when God means us to be princes. But, above all, we study this in order that we may assert a confidence and a certainty and a steadfastness in our Christian lives.

Now you will find, if you analyse these five verses, that the main things they display to our wondering gaze are these. First, they show us something of the origin and the plan of salvation; they then direct our attention to the One by whom the plan has been carried out, and this leads us into a consideration of the things that he has done, and eventually shows us the purpose and object of it all. There it is, then, the whole purpose and plan of salvation. And now, of course, we must start with the first thing. That sounds a trite, almost ridiculous remark, and, yet, as I have been trying to show, it is essential that we should start at the beginning. Strangely enough, the Christian gospel—let me say this with reverence, lest I be misunderstood—the Christian gospel does not start even with the Lord Jesus Christ, it starts with God the Father. The Bible starts with God the Father always, everywhere, and we must do the same, because that is the order in the blessed Trinity: God the Father, God the Son, God the Holy Spirit. You find that very thing emphasized and impressed here, for the statement is that salvation is entirely of God; this is the first thing we must always say when we begin to consider this question of salvation. Salvation is entirely of God, it is the gift of God: 'As thou hast given him power over all flesh, that he should give eternal life to as many as thou hast given him'—it is all there.

Let us therefore remind ourselves before we go any further that the gospel announces, at the very beginning, that man is absolutely helpless in the matter of his salvation, he can do nothing at all about it. The gospel is not a scheme or proposal to enable men to save themselves, nor is it a programme which God has outlined, an example of which has been given in the person of the Son of God, telling us how we can raise ourselves and lift ourselves into heaven. No, it starts by telling us that we cannot do it, we are all dead in trespasses and sins, we are utterly helpless, we are quite powerless, and while we were yet without strength Christ died for the ungodly. It was while man was in a state of complete bondage to sin and Satan and hell that God did something. Now that is the very essence of this message. It is impressed upon us here at the beginning, indeed, we find that our Lord goes on repeating it. The gospel is just the good news which tells us what God has done about us men, and about our salvation. I trust that no one still thinks of salvation as something that he or she has to arrive at for himself or herself. I hope nobody will think that church attendance, for instance, is going to gain them their salvation before God. That is a complete fallacy, for this message starts by saying that it is entirely and utterly of God, and comes solely from him.

'The wages of sin is death'—that is something that you and I have—'but the gift of God is eternal life through Jesus Christ our Lord' (Rom 6:23). That is how Paul says it, but our Lord says it here in the same way: 'As thou hast given him power over all flesh, that he should give eternal life to as many as thou hast given him.' This gospel of John has been saying it from the very beginning, it was the whole essence of the word to Nicodemus; you have to be *received*, then you have to be born again—it is all of God. 'God so loved the world, that he gave his only begotten Son . . .' The quotations are endless. But we must emphasize this at the very beginning. It is only as we begin to realize this that we can grasp something of the essential greatness of this salvation, that the great, almighty, eternal God should have done anything at all about it. But the message is that he has, and in the way that we are now going to consider.

It is, then, because of all that, that our Lord in his prayer here at the crucial moment, is concerned above everything else about glorifying God. 'Father,' he says, 'glorify thy Son, that thy Son also may glorify thee.' Now his main concern is not simply that *he* should be glorified. He is only concerned about that because of this greater thing: he is so anxious to glorify the Father that he wants the Father to glorify him, he wants the Father to glorify himself. This is, of course, one of the most stupendous things we can ever contemplate. Our Lord's one great desire throughout his life here on earth was to glorify his Father. He keeps on saying it. He has not come to do his own will, but the will of his Father who has sent him. He speaks the Father's words, he does the Father's works, and his one concern is that he may never fail him, that he may never falter in the great task that has been allotted to him. He lives entirely and exclusively to glorify his Father. He has not come to show himself, or to glorify himself. 'He humbled himself,' wrote the apostle Paul and that is the whole meaning of that term, for, in his abasing himself, he put himself as the Son in the Eternal Trinity, he glorified the Father; that was the whole purpose of his coming, and everything he has done was designed for that one and only supreme object—the glory of the Father, and, here, he prays for it.

But I cannot say a thing like that, of course, without deducing and adding that the whole purpose of your salvation and mine is that *we* should glorify the Father. Oh, that we might grasp this! I know that we are all guilty at this point— and I am as guilty as anybody else—of tending to think of God and the whole Christian salvation as something to solve our problems. People come and talk to me, and it is generally put in that way: 'What will salvation do for me?' they ask. And the answer that is given so often in our evangelism is, 'Believe the gospel, and it will do some marvellous things for you.' I say, thank God that that is true, but, my dear friends, we should not put that first. The ultimate aim and object of our salvation is that we may glorify God. The essence of sin is that we do not glorify God—let us be quite clear about this; the essence of sin does not lie in the particular acts or actions of which you and I and others may be guilty. Now that is where we go wrong. We think of sin in terms of particular sins and that is why respectable people do not think they are sinners. They utterly fail to realize that the essence of sin is not to glorify God, and anybody who does not glorify God is guilty of sin of the foulest kind. Even though you may never have got drunk, though you may never be guilty of adultery, if you live for yourself and your own glory you are as desperate a sinner as those other people whom you regard as sinners. That was put very plainly by the prophet Daniel to King Belshazzar in Daniel 5, when he pointed out to him that the essence of sin was not that he put wine in the holy cups of God and drank out of them with his wives and concubines, but that he had not humbled himself before the Lord, he had exalted himself and not given God the glory.

We can put this principle very briefly in this way. The first question in the shorter Catechism of the Westminster Confession is, 'What is the chief end of man?' and the answer is, 'The chief end of man is to glorify God and to enjoy him for ever.' So that I assert that the essence of salvation is to bring us into the state in which we *do* glorify God. It does not matter what is happening, or what goes wrong for us, we are meant to glorify him and live thus to his glory. It is the object of salvation from which, therefore, I deduce this final principle, that the ultimate proof of the fact that we are Christians is that we desire to do that. The final proof of our

salvation is not that we are happy whereas formerly we were
unhappy. Christian Science or the cults can do that, and so
can psychotherapy. These can take the miserable, and those
who are worried and anxious, and can give them treatment
so that they find that all their problems vanish and they are
perfectly happy and contented; they have merely been able to
forget their troubles and have undergone some change in
their life. If that alone is the test of salvation, well then, I have
nothing to say to the cults or to psychology.

But that is not the essential proof of salvation. The essential proof is that the supreme object and ambition of the
Christian's life now is to live to the glory of God. If we say
that when a man is saved he becomes a partaker of the divine
nature, that he is born again, and that Christ dwells in him,
then it follows that a Christian is a man who becomes pro-
gressively more and more like the Lord Jesus Christ. And
when I look at him this is what I find: I find that he was a
man of sorrows and acquainted with grief. He had great and
terrible temptations pressing upon him, but I find that in all
circumstances, and in all places, he had but one great desire
and that was to live to the glory of God. Christianity is not
something light and superficial that just does certain things
to you, and gives you certain pleasant feelings. It is something that brings you into a relationship with God. You
begin to fix your gaze on him, and to be awed by his holiness. You approach him with reverence and godly fear, you
do not drop lightly into his presence. No, you address him,
as his Son did, as Father, holy Father, righteous Father, and
over and above what may happen, and over and above your
feelings of salvation, is this deep desire to live to his glory, to
display it, to give yourself to it—the glory of God.

I want to take it a step further, in this way—the chief end
of salvation is, as I say, that God may be glorified and that
his glory may be displayed and acknowledged. The result of
that is that it is the gospel of salvation that really reveals to us
the *glory* of God. Our Lord puts that in the form of a

petition. Here he is, just before the cross, the crucial moment is at hand. He knows something about the agony and the sweat of Gethsemane, and his one desire is this: Father, enable me to go on, give me strength to bear, give me all I need to do this, in order that your great glory in this matter of salvation can be revealed and made manifest. I have come to do that, enable me to do it that your name may be glorified. That is his petition, that is his plea.

How, then, does the gospel of Jesus Christ thus manifest the glory of God in a way that nothing else does? Again I would remind you that that is his chief purpose. Even before he is concerned about saving us, he is concerned about revealing the glory of God. Have you realized that, or have you always thought of salvation only as something that is meant to save men? It does do that, of course, but before that, it is meant to display the glory of God. It does so first of all by revealing the character of God. The gospel of Jesus Christ displays, in a way that nothing else does, the *holiness and the righteousness* of God; the whole plan and scheme of salvation proclaims the fact that God cannot ignore sin. God cannot say, 'Well, I will pretend I have not seen it; yes, they have sinned and gone astray and rebelled against me, but I am a loving Father, I do not see things like that, it is all right, I will have them back.' No, the gospel plan of salvation tells us that God—I say it with reverence—cannot do that. The holiness and the righteousness of his eternal being and character mean that he cannot ignore sin. Sin is a reality, a problem (I say it again with reverence), even to God. It is something he sees and has got to deal with, and so he displays the glory of his being in his holiness and righteousness.

But thank God he does not stop at that, for the next thing he does is to reveal his *benignity*, his *mercy* and his *compassion*. You start with sin and the holiness of God, but if you leave it at that, if that were all, there would be very little difficulty about knowing what God would have done. He would simply have blotted out man from the world. He could have done it so easily—he could have consigned all the world, and all its designs, to perdition and eternal torment, and he would have been utterly justified in doing so. But the gospel tells us that he has not done so, he has done the opposite— why?—it is because of his benignity, because of his mercy, which means his pity, for us, his sorrow for us, because of his compassion.

We shall be seeing later on how our Lord displayed all this in his own personal life. How often do the evangelists tell us that he looked upon and had compassion upon some poor suffering person? It is because he was like his Father; the glory of God's character is thus revealed in the gospel. He does not destroy our world, but rather he does something else—and this leads me to his wisdom. Paul was very fond of emphasizing this when he addressed the clever philosophers at Corinth and others, too. Christ, he says, is the power of God, and the wisdom of God, and nowhere is the wisdom of God so gloriously and magnificently displayed as in this Christian gospel. Let me explain this. Here is man in sin, there is God in the heavens. God must recognize this and yet because of his character he does not blot us out. He is going to do something about it because of his mercy and compassion. How is he going to do it? The answer is the plan of salvation, this way that God employed, in his amazing wisdom. He sent his Son, and the Son came through the whole miracle of the virgin birth; he took human nature unto himself and lived as a man—the wisdom:

> Oh loving wisdom of our God!
> When all was sin and shame,
> A second Adam to the fight
> And to the rescue came.
>
> *J. H. Newman*

I am simply noting these things in passing. Have you ever stood in amazement as you have contemplated the loving *wisdom* of our Lord as displayed and revealed in the plan of salvation? Oh, we must go back to these things! We must come and look at the plan, its whole conception and the carrying out of it, and behold the perfection of the plan, contemplate, dwell upon it, meditate upon it, forget everything else for a while and give ourselves to this.

But not only that, I want to emphasize the way in which the gospel displays the great *love* of God. You notice I draw a distinction between the benignity, the mercy and compassion, and the love of God. I feel we must do that, for, after all, the love of God is displayed in particular in this matter of salvation, in his actual sending of the Son, his sparing him, if I may so put it, from the courts of heaven. My dear friends, God is no philosophic concept! God is a person and, as a person, God is, and God loves, and the essence of the life of the blessed Trinity is the love of the Father to the Son and the Spirit, and the love of the Son to the Father and the Spirit, and the love of the Spirit to the Father and the Son. We cannot conceive of that perfect unity, that perfect bliss, that absolute love, and yet it is all found in salvation. 'God so loved the world that he gave . . .'—yes, and I put it negatively, too, as Paul puts it in writing to the Romans: 'He that spared not his own Son.' It is there, you see, the love of God, in that he sent the Son of his love, the only begotten Son, into this cruel, sinful world; allowed him to live life in that way as a man, and allowed him to suffer 'such contradiction of sinners against himself'. And he placed your sins and mine upon him on the cross in such a way that at that moment Father and Son were separated, and the Son cried out, 'My God, my God, why hast thou forsaken me?' When I believe that that is possible within the Father-heart of God, then I cannot believe the doctrine of the impassivity of God. I say that God in his love suffered in his Son, and it is there I see the marvellous love of God displayed. And this great gospel manifests, too, the glory of God in revealing his character in this way.

But we should see also the way in which this plan of

salvation reveals the *justice* of God. God, because he is righteous and holy cannot, even in his love, do anything that is unjust. God, says Paul in Romans 3, must find a way of salvation which enables him at one and the same time to be just, and the justifier of the ungodly. If God forgave sin without still ministering his own justice, he would no longer be God. The marvel of this plan is that God, in putting our sins on Christ and dealing with them and punishing them there, can forgive us, and still be just. He has punished sin, he has not forgotten or ignored it. What happens in salvation is not that God says, Ah, they have sinned, I ought to punish them, but after all that would be rather hard. No, he does it through the Son, in the way I have outlined, and he is just. So the plan of salvation displays to us the glory of God's being by showing us the justice and absolute rightness of his holy character.

And, finally, it displays to us, again in a way that nothing else does, the *power* of God. The power of God was manifested in the incarnation when he prepared a body for his Son and worked the miracle of the virgin birth—what a marvellous power! But not only that. I rather prefer to think of it like this: it is as we look at God in Christ and all that he did in him through this plan of salvation, that we see his complete power to master everything that is opposed to himself, everything that is opposed to the best interests of man and everything that is opposed to the best interests of this world.

For the fact is that the whole problem has arisen in this way. One of the brightest of the angelic beings that were created by God, rebelled against God, and raised himself up against him. That is the origin of Satan. He is a power, a person, an angel of great might. He is as great as this: that he deluded a man and conquered him, thereby making himself the god of this world, and the 'prince of the power of the air' (Eph 2:2). There has never been a man in this world who has been able to stand up to beat him in fight and in combat. The power of the devil is something that we seriously underestimate, for he is such a power that he does not feel ashamed to pit himself against God himself. He verily believed he had overturned all the work of salvation when the Son of God went to the cross.

But, says Paul in Colossians 2, it is there he made his greatest blunder, for by the cross God, 'spoiled principalities and powers, he made a shew of them openly, triumphing over them in it' (verse 15). Christ met Satan face to face in single combat and routed him; at the cross he fulfilled the promise given to man at the beginning, when Adam was told that the seed of the woman should bruise the serpent's head—it was in the plan of salvation. Ultimately, therefore, the power of God is a great power to rout Satan and all his cohorts, and it assures us that finally he will be cast into the lake of fire and every evil will be destroyed and burnt out of existence.

We see thus, at the very beginning of this prayer, that the primary object of this great and wondrous gospel is to display the glory of God. 'Father, the hour is come; glorify thy Son, that thy Son also may glorify thee.' How much time do we spend in contemplating this glory, in looking at it? Oh, let us study it! Let us forget ourselves and our moods and states and feelings and desires, and just stand back for a moment and meditate upon it. Let us contemplate the plan and the scheme of salvation and feel ourselves lost in wonder, love and praise.

4

Our Security in God

John 17:1–5

In our study of this great chapter we have been concentrating in particular upon the great doctrine of salvation as it is revealed and displayed to us in these five verses. So far we have seen that the entire glory for salvation must go to God, and we have been looking at this truth in general. We have seen how the plan of salvation manifests God's great character, his holiness, his mercy, his wisdom, his love, his justice and his power. We have just noted these things, but we know that as we go on and follow what we are told here, and particularize a little more, we shall see the glory of God in a still more wonderful manner. Now I trust that no one is doubtful as to the importance of this consideration. I hope there is no one who is thinking, 'All this would be fine if one had leisure and nothing else to do. It is quite all right to be considering the glory of God and meditating upon it, but speaking for myself, I find life very difficult and trying. I am hard pressed. All my energies have to go to making a living. I have problems in my own life. I have sickness in the family. I am literally hemmed in by difficulties of all kinds and forms. What has all this to do with me?'

So often men in their ignorance and folly have taken up that position. They have regarded this wonderful doctrine of the glory of God as something theoretical and remote. But, my dear friends, there is no greater fallacy than that! The very fact that our Lord offered this prayer proves in and of itself how completely foolish that is. Why did he offer that prayer, and especially why did he offer it audibly? There is only one answer to that question: he was concerned about these disciples. He had to leave them. He was no longer going to be with them in the flesh, and he reminded his Father, in this prayer, of what he had done for them while he was with them. But now, he continues, 'I am no more in the world, but these are in the world, and I come to thee' (verse 11), and he makes known what his desire is for them. His desire for them is that they may come into such a knowledge of their relationship to God that in spite of the fact that he is going to leave them, and in spite of the fact that the world is going to hate and persecute them, they will not be shaken.

There was never anything more practical than this, because the only ultimate strength and hope and consolation that the Christian gospel offers to anybody in this world is just that of understanding the plan of salvation and knowing our relationship to God. And there is no question about this in practice. I have certainly observed during many years in the Christian ministry and as a pastor that, generally speaking, most of the problems and difficulties which people have are due to the fact that they have not taken a firm hold of this great doctrine. As we have seen, it is subjectivity that accounts for our troubles, because we only look to ourselves. But once a man sees himself as part of this great plan, most of his problems are solved almost automatically. So that is why we are going on to consider some of the detailed aspects of the plan of salvation as it is revealed in these five verses in particular.

Having said that the plan of salvation reveals the character of God, I want to put to you, as my next proposition, that salvation is something which has been entirely planned by God, and that this is something which is suggested here on the very surface: 'Thou hast given him power over all flesh,

that he should give eternal life . . . I have finished the work
which thou gavest me to do.' That is the first thing, therefore, that we have to take hold of. Salvation, if we may so
put it, is entirely the idea of God; it emanates from and has its
source and origin in God the Father. Now this is a staggering
thought! So often you and I feel we have to placate God
because of sin, sin in us, sin in our mind and whole outlook
and thought, and sin in the world. We tend to think of God
as being opposed and antagonistic to us, and therefore we are
always thinking of him as someone we have to appease and
placate. We regard God as Someone who is unwilling to be
kind and gracious to us and to love us. We think of him as
Someone in the far distance in his eternal glory and absolute
righteousness who is not well disposed towards us. We feel
we have to put forward these great efforts in order to get him
to look upon us with favour.

That is a complete fallacy. Salvation has all originated in
the mind of God—it is God's own purpose. I go so far as to
say that even the Lord Jesus Christ does not have to placate
God. Sometimes our hymns can be rather dangerous, and
there are certain of them that would lead us to the conclusion
that the Son of God has to plead with the Father to have
mercy and pity upon us. But that is a gross misunderstand-
ing of the term 'Advocate', it is something that is absolutely
foreign to biblical teaching. Rather, the Bible teaches that
'God was in Christ, reconciling the world unto himself, not
imputing their trespasses unto them' (2 Cor 5:19); 'God so
loved the world, that *he gave* his only begotten Son . . .' (Jn
3:16). It is all from God. So this idea that the Lord Jesus
Christ is at great pains to persuade God the Father to forgive
and accept us is utterly unscriptural and entirely false; the
source and origin of salvation is the great and eternal heart of
God.

But we go from that to this further point. It is not only
God's idea, we see here that it has been perfectly planned
from the very beginning to the very end. Here we come to

something that is the source of the deepest assurance and consolation that any Christian person can ever know in this world of time. What could be more comforting and reassuring than the fact that there is nothing contingent about this salvation, nothing accidental, nothing that needs modification? It is a perfect plan. God has planned it from eternity, before the foundation of the world, it is eternally in the mind of God. There is nothing, therefore, that is accidental about this. It never needs to be modified, or changed or altered in any respect. Here again is a point at which so many have gone astray. There are those who believe and even teach— you will find it in the case of a certain well-known Bible— that God sent his Son into this world to found and establish a kingdom, but because the Jews rejected him, God had to modify his plan; he had to introduce this way of salvation and so the church was brought into being and ultimately, at some future time, the kingdom will be introduced. They believe that it was all a modification of God's original plan. But that, I say, is a theory without the slightest vestige of a basis in Scripture. Scripture, rather, teaches that this plan was worked out before the foundation of the world, before a single man was ever born. And we find this here in these words. 'Father, the hour is come.' What hour? The hour that God had determined. You see that the whole purpose is to be found in that one word—'the *hour*'. We shall return to this, so for the moment I merely note it in passing, in order to deduce from it this great truth that the plan of God is absolutely complete, and was complete, even before the world was created.

But let us just glance at this time element in order that we may have it firmly in our minds. The plan was there, but it has been revealed in parts, and the great emphasis in the Bible is that everything is always, absolutely on time, with never a second or a moment's delay. Every item has been fixed, everything happens at its appropriate moment. The promise at the beginning was given at the right moment, the flood came at a particular point, and warning was given to mankind: 'My spirit shall not always strive with man' (Gen 6:3). He is still doing the same now, but there is an end, there is a limit to it. A time is coming when God will judge the world, and he fixes a time when it is to happen. The call of Abraham was not something accidental, it was done at a precise moment. It was to Abraham that the statement was made that certain things should not happen until the iniquity of the Amorites should be completed. The going down to Egypt was not accidental, it was prophesied, and Abraham was told exactly how long they would be there—430 years— before it ever happened. All these things were perfectly planned because God has his time, God has his exact moment.

But let us come to Moses, to whom the promise was given just at the time when it was necessary, and, again, the promise was given to David in his day. You certainly find this argument employed in the writings of the prophets. They foretell these things with a minuteness and an exactness which to the natural man is quite astonishing, but when we realize that it was God who laid down that great plan in eternity—that everything was determined and everything planned so that things should happen in order for this great design—there is no difficulty at all about it. To anybody who realizes this, it is rather what you would expect, and it is exactly what you find in the Scriptures. And then, of course, there is the well-known verse in Paul's epistle to the Galatians: 'When the fullness of the time was come, God sent forth his Son, made of a woman, made under the law . . .' (Gal 4:4).

Now people often ask the question—'Why didn't Christ come earlier? Why did he come at that particular point?' Well, though we cannot answer this question in detail, we can say that there are many reasons why that was the right time. God had given his law to his own people. Men always want to claim that they can save themselves, so God gave

them time to see and understand that they cannot do so. He
gave them a perfect law and said, If you keep that you will be
saved; you will be righteous in my sight. He allowed them
to try to do that for at least fourteen centuries, but they failed
completely. And he also allowed the great succession of
Greek philosophers to come and put their thoughts before
man. Men said, 'Give us the right idea and we will carry it
out.' They tried to, but they failed. The same thing happened with the Romans and their legal system—all that had
been tried and failed before God's hour arrived, the hour that
had been planned in eternity.

I commend this to you as a fascinating study, apart from
the wonderful spiritual truth. As you read through the Old
Testament try to put yourself in the position of that anicent
race and you will often feel that God had forgotten his own
people and his plan of salvation. But every time you begin to
think that, and feel that the enemy was triumphant all along
the line, God does something again, and you will find that it
is not only the exact moment but also the exact thing for the
exact moment. It is always the case—and there is nothing
that is so comforting as this thought—'The Lord reigneth; let
the earth rejoice'; 'The Lord reigneth; let the people tremble'
(Ps 97:1;99:1). We must get hold of this truth that the whole
plan is already made in the mind of God. It is because of this
that the Son of God can turn to his Father at this particular
point and say, 'Father, the hour is come', the hour that we
originally agreed about is at hand. He had been preparing his
disciples for it, as we see, both in John 12 and even earlier
than that at the wedding in Cana, when he said, 'Mine hour
is not yet come.' The time was all determined, and planned.

But we do not stop at that—thank God for this—for the
end is likewise planned and certain. There are many
Christian people today who are asking questions. Why does
God allow the church to languish? Why does he allow certain things to happen in the church? Why does he allow this
liberal criticism of the Bible that has been going on for a

hundred years? Why doesn't he put a stop to all this? Well, that is not God's way, but there is one thing about which we can be certain, and that is that God reigns; and those who may be perplexed about the state of the church here or anywhere else under the sun need not trouble and worry and vex their righteous souls. God reigns! God is still seated there in the heavens and he looks upon the citizens of the earth as grasshoppers. What he has determined is going to be carried out; the hour and the end of history and the world is determined. God knows it, but nobody else knows the hour, says Christ, no, no man, not even the Son, but the Father only and he knows it. And if you are not comforted and encouraged by that, well I doubt whether you are a Christian at all. The consolation of the glorious biblical affirmations— that neither death nor life nor anything else can separate us from the love of God—rests upon the fact that everything is purposed and planned in the mind of God who sees the end from the beginning and whose power is such that no one can withstand it. He can even take up a man like Pharaoh and use him like clay to bring his own great purpose to pass.

So let us now, with reverence, look into this plan in a little more detail. I like to take a glimpse into it and I am going to do something now that some of you may regard as strange and odd. I am going to ask you to come with me and look into the Council that was held in eternity, the great Council that was held between the Father and the Son and the Holy Spirit. What was it all about? It was about this very question of salvation, and what happened there was that the Son, the second Person in the blessed Trinity was given an assignment; he was appointed the heir of all things. See him reminding his Father of that eternal Council here: 'As thou has given him [the Son] power over all flesh, that he should give eternal life to as many as thou hast given him . . .' Let us look into these things with wondering gaze, with amazement and astonishment and remember, as we are doing it, that we are really in a sense still thinking about ourselves, because that Council was held with respect to us.

So the first thing we see here is that contemplating what was going to happen to man and to the world, seeing the entry of sin and the fall, this eternal Council decided what should be done about it. And the first great decision was that this matter should be handed over specifically to the Son. It is the purpose of God, says Paul in Ephesians 1:10, that all things should be wound up in Christ, 'that in the dispensation of the fullness of times'—you see the time element again —'he [the Father] might gather together in one all things in Christ, both which are in heaven, and which are on earth; even in him.' In other words, the Lord Jesus Christ, in that Council, was appointed as the head of mankind. He was made responsible for the world, a kind of head and representative of all the earth and its peoples. He himself told us this at the end after he had risen, when he said to the disciples: 'All power is given unto me in heaven and in earth' (Mt 28:18).

Now this is one of those crucial principles which we must never fail to understand, one which throws great light upon many an obscure incident in the Old Testament which otherwise cannot be understood. Take, for instance, those appearances to men of the so-called 'Angel of the Lord'. There can be no question at all but that these are the appearances of the Lord Jesus Christ—what are called the 'theophanies'. He was interested in the world even then; it had all been given to him; that was why the world came to be created, it was in him and through him and by him. He is the One in eternity who is deputed to do this particular task. And the record, in a sense, is the record of our Lord carrying out this great task that had thus been given to him. That is the explanation, too, of John's vision in Revelation 5. John is perplexed that no one is big enough or strong enough to open the books—the books of history—then suddenly he sees the Lion of the tribe of Judah stepping forward and the whole of heaven seems to applaud. At last there is One who

OUR SECURITY IN GOD

OUR SECURITY IN GOD 61

is big enough and strong enough to take complete charge of history and to break the seals and to open the books. He is the Lord of history, yes, it has already been given to him, and it belongs to him.

So, then, we must look at it like this, that everything with respect to this world and to man has been handed over to the Lord Jesus Christ. He has been given this authority, this power over all flesh. He rules and reigns and controls everything that is in the world—the sun, the moon and the stars, the rivers and the streams—that is why he can hold back or send the rain and the thunder storms. He can produce an earthquake. He is controlling everything, for everything has been put into his hands. He is the Governor of the earth. He is in charge of the kingdom and he will remain in charge right on to the end when, according to Paul in 1 Corinthians 15, he will finally finish the work, and hand the kingdom back to his Father.

But I must not stop at that. God had not only, in that eternal Council, handed over the world and its powers to the Son, he has also given him a people. I wonder how often you have stopped to consider the second verse of this chapter of John, and how often you have battled with its tremendous doctrine? I wonder what you have made of it. 'As thou hast given him power over all flesh, that he should give eternal life to as many as thou hast given him.' Does he say, 'As thou hast given him power over all flesh, that he should give eternal life to all flesh'? No—'that he should give eternal life to *as many as thou hast given him*'. The universal and the particular are both here in one verse. This is indeed high doctrine, so high that no human can understand it, but so high and glorious, that every man who has the mind of Christ in himself, bows before it in humble reverence, in amazement and in astonishment.

Scriptural teaching is that while God has given to his Son power over all flesh, without any limits whatsoever, he has in particular given him a special people who are to enjoy the

blessings of Christian salvation and eternal life. He has to
give eternal life to as many as God the Father has given him,
but what I am emphasizing here is that it is God the Father
who has given him these people. He gave him these particular people who are coming into the church and into eternal
life, from the very beginning to the very end. All of them
were given to the Son, there in that eternal Council. It is God
who chooses them, and, according to John 6, it is God who
draws them to him, for unless, Jesus says, God does draw
them to him, they will never come. 'All that the Father
giveth me shall come to me; and him that cometh to me I
will in no wise cast out . . . And this is the will of him that
sent me, that every one which seeth the Son, and believeth
on him, may have everlasting life: and I will raise him up at
the last day' (Jn 6:37,40).

This is something that you find running right through
these Scriptures. God, from before the creation of the world,
had chosen these people. He gives these particular people to
his Son, and he says, I give them to you for you to save them
for me. 'Those whom thou hast given unto him'—that was
another decision of this great and eternal Council.

But, you see, it is even more particular than that, for God
the Father prescribes the particular work the Son has to do in
order to save these people. The Lord says, 'I have glorified
thee on the earth: I have finished the work which thou gavest
me to do.' I propose to come back to this again and to look at
it in more detail, but all I am emphasizing at this point is that
the work of saving these individuals was given by the Father
to the Son. Thus we find our Lord constantly saying that he
does nothing of himself. He says in effect, 'I am simply
doing the work which the Father has shown me and given
me to do.' It all comes from God the Father, who then sends
the Son into the world to do it—to give the Father back the
glory that the Son had with him before he ever sent him. But
it was God the Father who sent him, for 'God so loved the
world that he gave his only begotten Son'—his Son, with

power to save. And the purpose of it all, I would remind you again, was that you and I might become the children of God; that we might have this eternal life which is to know God, the only true and living God, and Jesus Christ whom he has sent into the world in order to bring us to this blessed knowledge.

My dear friends, are we not guilty of neglecting this glorious doctrine of the glory of God and the plan of salvation in eternity? Evangelical Christians, how often have *you* meditated about these things? Do you not think that we have been guilty of judging particular aspects of salvation instead of regarding this glorious plan? This is why we are so superficial and why we are so shaken in our faith when adversity comes to try us. Our faith is not sufficiently broadly based—we must go back into eternity.

Let me summarize the message by putting it like this— what I deduce from this doctrine is that the eternal God knows us and is interested in us and has a plan for us. If that is not enough for you, then I despair! The astounding thing I find here is that the eternal and absolute God knows me, that he thought of me before the foundation of the world, not only before I was born, but before he even made the world; that this eternal, absolute Being is interested in me, even me, as an individual and as a person, and that I was in his mind when he conceived this amazing plan that includes the incarnation and the cross, and the resurrection and the ascension, and the reign of his Son at his side that is going on now. What a staggering, yes, but what a glorious thought!

The next thing I deduce is that there is therefore nothing uncertain about my acceptance with God, nor about my forgiveness, nor about my sonship. When I realize that I have been brought into God's plan I know that nothing can frustrate this. Now there are many people who talk about the Protestant Reformation, and the influence it had upon the world. You find that certain statesmen do this. They say you cannot explain the history of England apart from the

Protestant Reformation. Neither, they say, can you explain the United States of America apart from these things, because they all had their origin in that Reformation. But how little do these people really see what it all means and what it really represents, which is that these great truths are absolute and certain. Do you know why the Pilgrim Fathers made that attempt, and succeeded in crossing the Atlantic? What was it that enabled men to do things like that, and to do things which were even more hazardous? It was that they believed in what is called the 'Doctrine of the Perseverance of the Saints', it was because they had seen themselves in the plan of God which cannot be broken and which cannot fail. It is as absolute as God, himself; he knows the end as well as the beginning. 'Neither shall any man,' said Christ, 'pluck them out of my hand.' It is unthinkable.

So the next deduction is: if God has done all this for us in Christ, and especially in his death, we can be certain that he will carry on with the work until it is completed. That is Paul's argument: 'He that spared not his own Son, but delivered him up for us all, how shall he not with him also freely give us all things?' (Rom 8:32). 'If, when we were enemies, we were reconciled to God by the death of his Son, much more, being reconciled, we shall be saved by his life' (Rom 5:10). Let me put it like this: God, who is sufficiently concerned about me to send his Son to die on the cross of Calvary for me, is not going to let me down when any difficulty or temptation faces me. My dear friends, there is *nothing* for you to fear! You belong to One of whom we are told that all power has been given to him over all flesh. You are in the hands of the Lord Jesus Christ if you but knew and realised it, and he controls everything. He controls every human being, all the affairs of nature, he is even controlling the devil himself. All power is given unto him, thrones, dominions, principalities and powers are subject unto him, so you need never fear! You and I have but to realize that we are in those mighty hands, that that strong arm is engaged on our behalf, that all flesh is under his power, and that all authority in heaven and on earth has been given to him.

Therefore, when you are troubled and perplexed and harrassed, and when all things seem to be against you and you despair, when you pray to him, before you say a word, just remind yourself of his authority and of his power: 'As thou hast given him power over all flesh . . .' He that has formed you has a power like that, and therefore, being in his safe keeping, why should you fear man or beast or the powers of nature or of hell? Simply trust in him, he has so loved you that he has died for you, and his power on your behalf is indisputable.

5

The Lord Jesus Christ, the Lord of Glory

John 17:1–5

We have been considering the way in which we see in these five verses the particular glory of the Father being revealed in salvation, and now we take a step forward and come on to consider the way in which our salvation has actually been produced. We have looked at it in the eternal Council and as God planned it, and as he set aside and separated his Son for the work. We now look at something of the detail of the way in which this was planned and conceived and was put into practice, so that we are looking especially at the glory of God in salvation as it is revealed in the person of the Son. And again, the same thing will strike us, namely, this emphasis upon the *glory*. It all has to do with the glory of the eternal Godhead. We have seen the glory of the Father, and we are now looking at the glory of the Son, and here again in an extraordinary manner we have before us this wondrous panorama, as it were, of the whole movement of salvation with regard to the Son himself.

Now this is something which is staggering not only to the mind but even to the imagination. The whole sweep of salvation is unfolded here and displayed before us from glory back to glory and it is all in the compass of these few verses. So we approach a subject like this with a sense of awe and wonder and adoration.

And as we do so, shall we not honestly admit that perhaps one of the greatest lacks in our modern Christianity—and here I speak not only of the church in general, but also, if we are to be quite honest, even of many of us who claim to be evangelical—that perhaps the greatest lack in our worship and practice of the Christian faith is the absence of a sense of wonder, a sense of adoration and a sense of worship. I have no doubt at all that this is very largely to be explained by the fact that we are so subjective. I have said this ever since we started considering this chapter, and I propose to go on saying it, because it seems to me to be one of the great lessons which we do need to learn especially at this present time. We are all too interested in our own moods and states and conditions; we are all too psychological and introspective, and too concerned, therefore, about the benefits that the Christian gospel and salvation have to give to us. And the result of this is that we miss something of these great glories of the gospel as it is unfolded in the New Testament itself. This comes out very clearly if we listen to one another; have you not noticed how there is a tendency to be talking about ourselves? We are always telling people what has happened to us. 'Testimony' today generally means what we have experienced, or what has happened to us. How rarely do we speak about him!

Now there is the lack and the need. If you read the lives of the saints who have gone before us in this world, you will find that they spent most of their time in talking together about Jesus Christ. Their testimony was a testimony to him, and to his praise. Their emphasis was upon him. They spoke about this wonderful Christ and the glory of his person, whereas we always tend to talk about ourselves, the things that we have found, the happiness that we have discovered, or some experience that we have had. And I think if we are honest we will find that the emphasis is always more or less centred upon self.

We have deviated very far indeed from what was so true

of the saints of the centuries. Take, too, your hymn books
and read the great hymns, especially, perhaps, the hymns
that were written before the middle of the last century. (The
subjective element seems to have come in just about then.)
Start with Isaac Watts and come down the great succession
and you will find they have this glorious objectivity. They
rejoiced in their experiences, yes, but the note you find outstanding in their hymns is always their praise of the Lord,
their glorying in *him*. With Isaac Watts they surveyed the
wondrous cross on which the Prince of glory died. That is
the predominant thought. They always spent their time in
worship and adoration and in the glorification of him.

It seems to me that this is the note that we must recapture,
and that there is no real hope for revival and true awakening
until we come back to this. And the way to do that is to
study the Scriptures, to spend our time in reading and meditating upon them and then in humbling ourselves in worship
and in adoration before such a marvellous truth. Now I am
saying this not merely in a theoretical manner for I am
anxious to be extremely practical. No, I advocate this
because, apart from anything else, the real cure for most of
our subjective ills is ultimately to be so enraptured by the
beauty and the glory of Christ that we will forget ourselves
and will not have time to think about ourselves at all. Now
that is a good bit of psychology. The trouble with our
generation, and let us not be too hard on ourselves, is that we
are living in a very difficult age. We have had to face problems which mankind has scarcely ever had to face in such an
acute form, and such an age always tends to produce mor-
bidity, a concern about oneself. We are living such a ridiculous type of life that our nerves are tired and frayed, and as a
result we are all of us concerned about self, and the great
problem is how to get away from it. The high road to that is
to be so absorbed by someone else, something outside oneself, which is so glorious and wonderful that, without knowing it, we forget all about ourselves. This can happen as you

look at some marvellous scenery, or fall in love and forget yourself; well, multiply that by infinity and look into the face of Jesus Christ and catch something of his glory, and I assure you that most of the 'mumps and measles of the soul' will automatically be cured, and you will find yourself in a healthy condition, mentally, spiritually and even psychologically.

But even more important than that is the fact that God has caused these Scriptures to be written in order that we may know something about this great salvation, 'so great salvation', as the New Testament describes it in Hebrews 2. I wonder whether we modern Christians realize the greatness of this Christian salvation as we ought, because if we do not, the way to do so is to learn something about the greatness of the glory of the person of our Lord and Saviour Jesus Christ. That is the way to measure the greatness of the salvation, not just by something that happens to us. Let us deliver ourselves from that! For if we are going to measure our salvation by what has happened to us, I suggest that finally we have no answer at all to give to the Christian Scientists, nor to the psychologists. If you make it subjective, you are still in the past. No, the way to measure the greatness of this salvation is to look at the greatness of the person and his glory and to realize something of what he has done.

Now this is the very thing that is shown to us in these verses. Look at the movement, beginning at verse 5: 'And now, O Father,' he says at the end of his earthly life, 'glorify thou me with thine own self with the glory which I had with thee before the world was.' That is the starting point. You just try to consider and contemplate this amazing and glorious person before he ever came to earth. You do not start with the babe in Bethlehem, that was not the beginning of his life. He *came* into this world, he was not born into it in the way that everybody else has been born into it. He came from the glory. He entered into this world from another world, and what he himself says here is precisely what is said everywhere else in Scripture, that he came out of the eternal, everlasting glory of the Godhead. He also says here that he shared that essential glory of the eternal God from all eternity —'Glorify thou me now with thine own self with the glory which I had with thee before the world was.'

Once again we must admit that we are trying to look at something which transcends the reason and the grasp of our finite minds. But it is the teaching of the Scriptures—the eternal triune God, the Father, Son and Holy Spirit, yet but one God, and this Son of God, the Second Person in the Trinity is sharing in all the fullness of that glory. As the author of the epistle to the Hebrews puts it, 'Who being the brightness of his glory, and the express image of his person' —that is the description of the Lord Jesus Christ. He is the effulgence of the glory of the Father, the express image of his person. Paul, in Philippians 2, expresses the same truth when he says, 'Who, being in the form of God, thought it not robbery to be equal with God.' He is, to use an old phrase, self-substantial, co-equal, co-eternal with the Father. He is the eternal Son in the eternal bosom of the Father, one with God, the Second Person in the blessed, holy Trinity. 'In the beginning was the Word, and the Word was with God, and the Word was God'—that is it. He shared in full the ineffable, indescribable glory of the eternal Godhead. That is the way you start thinking about the Lord Jesus Christ.

So, then, the next step, obviously, is this: he prays that God the Father will glorify him again with that glory which he had with him before the world was, the implication being that something has happened to that glory. And that is precisely the teaching of the New Testament. In order to become man he laid aside this eternal glory which he had with the Father in heaven. Let us be careful here, and let us be quite sure that we know exactly what we are saying. I am not saying that he laid aside his deity, because he did not. What he did lay aside was the glory of his deity. He did not cease to be God, but he ceased to manifest the glory of God.

Perhaps the best way of understanding this is to consider what happened on the Mount of Transfiguration when he was transfigured before Peter and James and John. A kind of radiance came upon him, surpassing anything that had ever been seen before by those disciples. Now contrast that with what he normally appeared to be. Or again, take the case of Saul of Tarsus going down to Damascus. He suddenly saw a light in the heavens brighter than the shining of the sun itself, and he saw it came from a face, that of this glorified Jesus of Nazareth (Acts 9). Now you see exactly what is described here.

Again, contrast that glory with what we are told about him when he was here on earth: 'There is no beauty that we should desire him . . . a man of sorrows, and acquainted with grief' (Is 53:2–3). People would look at him and say, Who is this fellow? 'Is not this the carpenter, the son of Mary?' (Mk 6:3). He had laid aside the glory, he had not laid aside anything of his essential being or person or of his essential deity. But neither had he held on to it, he had not clutched at the manifestation of his glory, he had laid that aside as one would a cloak and had come in the likeness of man. Indeed, I must go much further than this, because this is the wonder of it all. He decided that his glory should be veiled by flesh. Think of it like this: the glory is there still shining in all its power, but a veil of flesh has come over it so that mankind cannot see it. Take an Old Testament illustration. In the wilderness Moses went on to the Mount and spoke with God, and when he came down his face was shining. The people saw the glory and it was so bright that he had to put a veil over his face; the glory was still there but it was hidden from them. Something like that happened to our Lord. Yes, but he not only came as man, nor is it only true to say that his glory was veiled by flesh. It is not true to say simply that the eternal Son of God was made flesh. We are told that he was made 'in the likeness of sinful flesh' (Rom 8:3). Indeed, he not only came into this world as a man, he took on him the 'form of a servant' (Phil 2:7). It would have been a wonderful and astounding thing if this eternal King and Prince of glory had come on earth and lived in a palace as a human king with all the pomp and glory of an earthly kingship—but not at all! He was born as a babe in very poor circumstances. Mary and Joseph did not have the money to offer the usual offering. They could only offer two turtle doves when he was born. He worked as a carpenter and he had to earn his living. He did not have a home he could claim for himself, or a place to lay down his head. He took upon himself the form of a servant and was dismissed and derided by the so-called great ones of this world of time; he stooped as low as that from the height of the glory from which he had come. Thus here on earth, in a sense, he had not that glory and he asked his Father to restore that glory to him.

There is no better way of saying all this than to put it in the words of Charles Wesley's hymn—and how foolish we are to think that such hymns were only meant for special seasons of the year!

> Veiled in flesh the Godhead see!
> Hail, the Incarnate Deity.

or again:

> Mild, He lays His glory by;
> Born, that man no more may die.

Look at these paradoxes, these tremendous contrasts, but it is all the simple and literal truth. He thus mildly lays aside his glory and comes right down to earth, takes on human nature, lives as man in the likeness of sinful flesh and in the form of a servant. In these things we behold the amazing descent from the glory.

The next thing we are told is that we must look at his work here on earth, which really is that of glorifying the Father. He did this in many ways. He says here, 'I have glorified thee on the earth,' and in doing that, of course, he, in a sense, manifested his own glory, veiled in flesh. He revealed and declared the Father by just being what he was. He said on one occasion, 'He that hath seen me hath seen the Father' (Jn 14:9); look at him and you see something of the glorious God, the Father himself. You see the eye of compassion, the understanding, the readiness to help and to bless.

If only we could see the Father, said Philip on one occasion: 'Lord, shew us the Father, and it sufficeth us.'

And the Lord turned to him and said, 'Have I been so long time with you, and yet hast thou not known me, Philip? he that hath seen me hath seen the Father . . .' (Jn 14:8–9). In other words, he manifested the Father and the glory of the Father in his life and all his activities and in being what he was.

But then he also does the same thing, of course, in his teaching. There was never such teaching concerning God the Father as fell from the lips of our blessed Lord and Saviour Jesus Christ. Man's ideas of God are always incomplete and imperfect, even the Old Testament revelation was not enough. As the author of the epistle to the Hebrews puts it, God has revealed this truth concerning himself in parts here and there—'in time past unto the Fathers by the prophets'— but now he has revealed it in his Son, perfect, final, full and complete. It is all there in this wonderful person, the blessed Lord and Saviour Jesus Christ—and in all his teaching and all his references concerning the Father we find all this revealed.

But then he did it in a still more striking way by doing the work which the Father had sent him to do—'I have finished the work which thou gavest me to do'—and what was the work? First and foremost, he kept the law himself. God had given his law to mankind and he had told them to keep it, in order to glorify him. The whole spirit of the law is that we should glorify God; it is not merely to keep a number of rules and regulations, doing this and not doing that. The real object of the law is that mankind might be taught and shown how to glorify God. But mankind had failed, and so the first thing the Son was sent to do was to honour and keep the law, and thus to glorify God, and he did it perfectly. It was an essential part of his work.

Not only that, he came in order that he might be a perfect High Priest to represent those redeemed people whom God the Father had given to him. In Hebrews 5 we are told a very remarkable thing about our blessed Lord in that respect. We are told that 'learned he obedience by the things which he suffered'. The Lord Jesus Christ, the Lord of glory, had to be taught certain things before he could become a perfect High Priest and to represent us in the presence of God. He came into this world in order to be the Captain of our salvation, our Leader, and he had to be prepared for that work and to go through this process. He had to be tempted in all points even as we are in order that he might succour us when we are tempted and be a sympathetic and understanding High Priest. He came down from the realms of glory and submitted himself to all that, and as he was doing it, he was not only showing something of his own glory, he was showing us the glory of the Father who had ever planned such a way of salvation.

What an amazing and astounding thing this is! Oh, my friends, as we read these gospels we must always be reminding ourselves of that. Look at it in detail, look at the life of our Lord Jesus Christ and remember that this is the Lord of glory. Remember that this is the One who is the brightness of the Father's glory, the express image of his person. But look at him in the manger, or upon the Mount, suffering hunger and thirst; the Lord of glory, mildly laying by his glory and thus living life in this world as a man, being prepared to be the Captain of our salvation.

But now we come to one of the most remarkable things of all. In the first verse we read, 'Father, the hour is come; glorify thy Son, that thy Son also may glorify thee.' Is this the same petition as that in verse 5: 'And now, O Father, glorify thou me with thine own self with the glory which I had with thee before the world was'?

I suggest to you that it is not the same thing, and that the two petitions do not have reference to precisely the same matter. I think that the petition in verse 1 means that the hour is come, he is about to die, about to face the greatest crisis of all. Oh, it was a mighty thing, transcending thought and imagination, for him to leave that glory, to be born as a babe and to take unto himself human nature. It was a tremendous thing for the eternal Son of God to be lying in the womb of a woman. All his trials and difficulties are something that we will never grasp and never understand in this world. And deeper and greater and beyond it all was this trial that he was now about to endure, the cross and all that it meant. So here, living life as a man, he prays to the Father, 'Father, glorify thy Son', by which he means, Strengthen me, enable me to show and to give proof of the fact that I am your Son. Again, in Hebrews 5, we are told that he prayed with crying and strong tears unto God to hold him and strengthen him, and we are also told there that he was heard because of his reverence and godly fear, and his beautiful piety.

And this means that he realized what he was about to do. He realized that the moment was coming when the weight of the world's sins were to be put upon him, when he was to bear the staggering load of the guilt of the whole of mankind, that the Father had placed upon him, and it was an overwhelming thought. Would his human nature, as it were, crack and break under it? Could he stand this load, could he stand the thought of losing sight of his Father's face as he was made sin for man, and as he bore the sin and punishment of man? Father, he says, strengthen me, hold me, prove to the world that I am your Son, glorify your Son in this world. That is the meaning of the petition in the first verse, and the prayer was answered. Oh yes, he came from the highest heaven of glory, and, as I have reminded you, was born as man, made flesh, made in the likeness of sinful flesh. He took on him the form of a servant. He endured the contradiction of sinners against himself. And, as Paul says in Philippians 2, he became obedient unto death, even the death of the cross. He was crucified and nailed upon a tree, there is no deeper death than that—

> From the highest realms of glory
> To the Cross of deepest woe.

He asked that the Father would enable and strengthen him and his Father heard his prayer. He was glorified, he was strengthened and he was enabled, so that at the end he was able to say, 'It is finished.' He had borne it all; it had not crushed him; the body had not cracked under it. The work was done, he had accomplished everything: 'Father,' he said, 'into thy hands I commend my spirit.'

Then, secondly, comes the petition in verse 5. The Lord is still looking to what is before him, and this is his prayer. Having completed all the work, having done everything which the Father had appointed him to do, he asks, as it were: Has not the time now arrived when I can come back to you, exactly where I was before? I have done the work. 'Father, glorify thou me with thine own self with the glory which I had with thee before the world was.' But the astonishing thing for us to remember at this point is that he goes back as God-Man! In eternity he was God the Son, pure deity, and he shared the glory, but now he goes back as God-Man. And as God-Man, and our representative, the glory which he momentarily laid aside at the request of the Father is restored to him, and thus as God-Man and Mediator he again shares this ineffable glory of the eternal God.

And so this prayer, too, was answered. It began to be answered at the resurrection, the event which finally convinced even the disciples that he was the Son of God. They did not quite understand it before, but, as Paul puts it in writing to the Romans, our Lord was, 'declared to be the Son of God with power, according to the spirit of holiness, by the resurrection from the dead' (Rom 1:4). Who is this who has conquered death and the grave? He must be, he is, the Son of God. Consider the appearances after the resurrection. You find the disciples in Jerusalem behind locked doors because they were afraid of the Jews, and suddenly he came in without the door being opened. They thought it was a ghost. But he showed that he was not by asking them to give him something to eat. So they gave him 'a piece of a broiled fish and of an honeycomb'. 'You see who I am,' he says in effect, 'I have flesh and bones, and I can eat'—the glorious person of this risen Lord.

Then perhaps still more strikingly we see it in the ascension. Many of us do not observe Ascension Day, do we? We are a little inconsistent in this; we observe Christmas, Good Friday, and Easter Sunday! We observe Whit Sunday, but we do not observe Ascension Day, and it is a very essential part in all this movement of God's plan. His disciples were with him on the Mount and while he was speaking, he was lifted up and he ascended into heaven. His glory was manifested in a most amazing manner there. And then he manifested it still more by sending the gift of his Holy Spirit on the Day of Pentecost. It is a proof that he is the Son of God, the Messiah, this glorious being. And there he is now, sitting at the right hand of God in the glory, reigning until all his enemies shall be made his footstool.

And so I have tried to hold before you something of the glory which is depicted in these five verses, from the glory, down to the depths of the cross and to Hades, and back again via the ascension to that ineffable glory once more, and he now takes human nature with him. But why has he done all this? I can imagine someone saying, 'My dear Sir, this is all very well, you know. If we were living in a leisurely world and had no business and no cares and no worries and trials perhaps we could take all these remarks objectively. But we

want something that will help us now, here and now in the
immediate present, have you not something to say to us?'

I hope nobody feels like that after what we have just been
considering? I have just been reminding you of what the
eternal Son of God has done for you, that you might be
saved from the wrath of God and from hell, and from sin,
and from yourself. He has done it that you might become a
son of God, that you might begin to enjoy 'a joy unspeakable and full of glory', and that you might receive the Holy
Spirit with all his power and might. That is what it is all
about. If you feel that all I have been saying is something
theoretical and remote, it is because you do not understand,
because you are not related to it, and because you do not
realize it has all been done for you. That is the greatness of
the glory; he has done all this for us.

> From the highest realms of glory,
> To the Cross of deepest woe,
> All to ransom guilty captives
> Flow my praise, for ever flow.

And then I turn to him and say—

> Go, return, Immortal Saviour,
> Leave Thy footstool, take Thy throne,
> Thence return and reign for ever,
> Be the Kingdom all Thine own.

That is the true reaction to the things we have been considering together. He did it all to ransom guilty captives, and
if you realize that he has done that for you, you will agree
with Robert Robinson when he wrote these words: 'Is your
praise flowing? Do you praise the Lord Jesus Christ? Do you
praise him to other people; do you talk to them about him?'
People talk today about those whom they like and admire. I
read of them praising actors and actresses and all sorts of
politicians and people; you see it in the newspapers, and you
have to listen to them when you are trying to read in a

railway compartment. But do we praise the Lord Jesus Christ? If we do not it is because we do not realize what he has done for us. Again, I would agree with Robert Robinson when he says—'Break my tongue, such guilty silence.'

Oh, my dear friends, if you do not realize the glory of these things, hasten to God and confess it. Ask him so to give you his Holy Spirit that your eyes will be opened to these precious, glorious truths. The Holy Spirit was sent in order to make these things real to us. If we but realized these things then we would inevitably be praising with the whole of our being, and our whole life would be to his praise. The Holy Spirit will enable us to realize these glorious things. He will so imprint and impress them upon mind and heart and understanding that they will be real to us, so real that finally we shall be able to join Paul in saying, 'To me to live is Christ.'

6

Antidote to Introspection

John 17:1–5

We have been looking together in some detail at the first five verses in this chapter because we have suggested that in them we have a wonderful display of the scheme of salvation. I also suggested that it was good for us to be looking at this, because it is undoubtedly the most important thing that anybody can ever grasp in this life and world. The one message which the gospel of Jesus Christ has to give to the world outside the church is the message concerning the way of salvation. But we must never forget that it is also always the central message which is needed by the church herself, because we have considered together the fact that, even having believed the gospel, we often find ourselves spending our Christian life in what may be called 'shallows and miseries'. We often seem to be living a life which is full of problems and perplexities, without much happiness and joy, a life, as it were, of struggling, of barely succeeding and barely avoiding defeat. The main explanation of that, when it is true, is that in one way or another we have ceased to look at and to realize the truth about this great plan of salvation as it is unfolded in the Bible.

There can be no doubt at all but that one of the besetting temptations and sins of the average Christian is the tendency to be looking in a wrong way at oneself. Now it is true that

81

the Bible is full of exhortations to us to examine ourselves
and to prove ourselves, yes, but there is all the difference in
the world between doing that in the right way, and becoming introspective. You are introspective when you spend the
whole of your time looking at yourself, looking inward, and
being concerned only and supremely about yourself. The
antidote to that, I suggest, is that we look again at the plan of
salvation as it is unfolded in the Bible. And here, in this
chapter, in the brief compass of these first five verses, we
find it clearly summarized. There are many additional
reasons why we should always be doing this. One all important one for us to remember here is that it is only as we
remind ourselves of this plan, both in its various parts and as
a whole, that we shall not only be able to counteract certain
doubts that may arise in our own minds, but, still more
important, we shall also be able to answer those who attack
our position and attack the Christian faith from the outside.

Now it is no final answer to one of the most subtle attacks
upon the Christian faith today simply to say that we have
experienced certain things, or that we are in a certain position
now. Many people take up that argument and they often
imagine that it is a cogent one. They turn to the world and
say, 'You can say what you like about the Bible, you can
criticize the Christian faith as much as you like, but you
cannot make any difference to me because I am happy. The
gospel has done this and that for me and as a result I am quite
immune to all your criticisms.' I know what such friends
mean when they say something like that, but it seems to me
that it is not only putting the Christian position at the very
lowest, but there is also a sense in which it does not begin to
meet the attack made upon the faith. For the fact is, of
course, that if we are going to base our position solely upon
what we feel, and what we are at this moment, then we have
nothing to say to the attack thus made upon the Christian
faith, especially by psychology.

There are many today who would explain all our faith in

terms of psychology. They claim it as a very clever and subtle form of self-persuasion, just a way of shifting your difficulties on to another plane. 'It is good psychology,' they say, 'and anything that makes a man happier is a good thing, in and of itself; Christians may use all these great terms, but actually it is nothing but a bit of psychology. As you know, there are many false teachings, such as Christian Science, which are quite unjustifiable, but which can make people very happy.'

So, then, if we base our position entirely upon experience, we will convince nobody. The answer to the good psychology argument is that we are dealing with certain historical events and facts which we must never allow ourselves to forget. Indeed, I am prepared to go as far as to say that whatever I may feel at this moment, though I may feel that I am in a state of darkness and blackness, and am utterly discouraged, my position is still safe and I am secure because of these things that have been done in history outside of me and before I was ever born. Thank God I do not base my position on how I feel. Feelings are treacherous, they come and go, and what little control we have upon them! We have all had the following experience, have we not? We wake up one morning and find ourselves full of peace and joy and happiness, and all seems to go well. We have a marvellous day, we read our Bibles, we have freedom in prayer, and all is well, so we look forward to the next day being still more wonderful. But, strangely enough, we find that when we wake up the next morning we are lifeless and dull. If you are going to base your whole position upon experience and feelings, you are going to be a very unhappy person and your Christian life is going to be very unstable. But the answer is, I repeat, this marvellous plan of salvation. I must, of course, know that I am related to it—that is essential—but what I am arguing for is that if you want to enjoy these blessings and if you want to live this Christian life truly, you do so by looking at these things, by resting upon them and by saying, if you like, in the words of a hymn:

> My hope is built on nothing less
> Than Jesus' Blood and Righteousness,
> I dare not trust my sweetest frame,
> But wholly lean on Jesus' Name.
> On Christ the solid rock I stand,
> All other ground is sinking sand.
>
> *Edward Mote*

That, then, is what we are doing by looking together at the plan and scheme as it is here unfolded. So far we have seen something like this. We have seen that the great object and intent of the plan of salvation is the glory of God, and if we do not see that first and foremost, then there is something wrong with our whole conception of salvation. If we look at salvation only in terms of ourselves or of something that happens to us, and do not see in it primarily the glory of the almighty God, then our view of salvation is grossly inadequate, indeed, it may even be a false one. It is the glory and the wonder of the triune God which our Lord emphasized and he is our supreme authority.

Now we have been looking at the plan in its different parts. We have seen that it originates with the Father. He planned and purposed it, and set it into operation in the eternal Council. Then we have seen how the work was divided, the Son was sent, a commission was given to him, and he accomplished the work to the glory of God the Father. And he himself, as we were considering in our last study, was glorified in the resurrection and the ascension, but the final manifestation of the glory of the Son was that which was given on the Day of Pentecost when the Holy Spirit was sent down upon the infant church gathered together at Jerusalem. That is the final proof of the fact that Jesus of Nazareth is the only begotten Son of God. The Scripture talks about the 'promise of the Father': the Father had promised the Children of Israel in the old dispensation that he would send his Spirit. He keeps on saying that he is going to make a new covenant with them, that the day is coming when he will take out their stony heart, give them a heart of flesh, and pour out his Spirit upon them. That is the thing to which they were looking forward, and, in a sense, the work of the Messiah, the Deliverer, the Saviour, was to send this promise of the Father. And that is the very thing that happened on the Day of Pentecost when the Lord Jesus Christ sent the Holy Spirit.

Now the Scripture uses two terms. In one place it tells us that the Lord Jesus Christ sent the Holy Spirit, and in another place it tells us that God the Father sent the Spirit after listening to the prayer of his Son, but it is the same thing, since the Spirit proceeds from the Father and from the Son. What I particularly want to emphasize at this point, however, is that this teaching is included even in these five verses that we are looking at in John 17: 'These words spake Jesus . . .' and then he began to pray. 'These words' refers to the words that are recorded in chapters 14, 15 and 16 of this particular gospel, which are all to do with this promise of the coming of the Holy Spirit. Our Lord began to speak about this in chapter 14. He found that the disciples were crestfallen because he had said that he was going to leave them, so he told them, 'I will pray the Father, and he shall give you another Comforter, that he may abide with you for ever; even the Spirit of truth; whom the world cannot receive, because it seeth him not, neither knoweth him: but ye know him; for he dwelleth with you, and shall be in you' (Jn 14:16–17). And he proceeded to teach them about the coming of the Holy Spirit.

So here, you see, in John 17:1, the coming of the Holy Spirit is introduced as a part of this great and vital plan of salvation, and it is, of course, one of the most wonderful aspects of all. There, in the Council in eternity, as we have already seen, God the Father, God the Son and God the Holy Spirit spoke together and planned the salvation of man; the

Father reiterated the great scheme, and the Son accepted the
decision that he should be the one to carry out the plan; and
then it was equally decided that the Holy Spirit should complete what the Son had done for mankind. This is what is
sometimes called the 'economy of the Trinity', the division
of the work between the three Persons, and it is something
that appears very clearly right through the Scriptures. It appears, for example, in the very beginning, in Genesis, where
we are shown how the creation itself was the work of the
Trinity—'In the beginning God . . .' Then we are told that
'the Spirit moved . . .'; everything was made through the
Word, but in a sense the agency was still the Spirit.

However, what I am anxious to look at now is the way in
which this verse brings out the point. The Father sends the
Son, and the great business of the Son is to glorify the
Father. He says, 'I have glorified thee on the earth; I have
finished the work which thou gavest me to do.' For there is a
sense in which the Lord Jesus Christ never glorified himself.
That is why he laid aside his glory, and why he was not born
in a king's palace but in a stable. That, too, is why he took
upon himself the form of a servant; it was all to glorify the
Father. All his life as a man was in a sense lived just in this
way, in order that all the glory and power might be of God
the Father.

But here we are told another wonderful thing. After he
went back to heaven, he sent upon the church the Holy
Spirit, and the business and the work of the Holy Spirit is to
glorify the Son. Now this is a marvellous statement. We do
not see the Holy Spirit, he is invisible, and, in a sense, that is
because his work is to glorify the Son. Indeed, we read about
the Holy Spirit in John 16:14 the same thing that we read
elsewhere about the Son. Our Lord says that the Holy Spirit
does not speak of himself, but, 'He shall glorify me: for he
shall receive of mine, and shall shew it unto you.' We are
told precisely the same thing about the Son in relation to the
Father. Therefore, the great controlling thought we must

hold in our minds is that the chief work of the Holy Spirit is to glorify the Lord Jesus Christ.

In a sense, the final glorification of the Lord Jesus Christ was the coming of the Holy Spirit. We are told in John's gospel that the Holy Spirit was not yet come because Jesus was not yet glorified. We see this in the great promise our Lord made one day in the Temple when he said, 'If any man thirst, let him come unto me, and drink. He that believeth on me, as the scripture hath said, out of his belly shall flow rivers of living water' (Jn 7:37–38). And John expounds that: 'This spake he of the Spirit, which they that believe on him should receive: for the Holy Ghost was not yet given; because that Jesus was not yet glorified.' So the Holy Spirit could not be given until Christ had finished the work the Father had given him to do, until he had died and risen again, until he had ascended and taken his seat at the right hand of God. God then said, in effect, 'I give you the promise, you send it upon the people.'

Now this is something that can be worked out in many different ways. I want to do it here in a more or less objective manner, but the subjective part is important in this way: If you claim that you have received the Holy Spirit in his fullness, then the best test of that is whether or not you are glorifying the Lord Jesus Christ. There is a danger that again we put such emphasis upon the Spirit himself that we do so at the expense of the Son. There are some people who are always talking about phenomena in the Christian life. They like talking about the gifts of the Spirit and boasting that they possess one or other of them: 'Do you speak in tongues? Have you got the gift of healing?' Their talk always seems to be about these things. Well, thank God, the Holy Spirit does give these gifts, but let us never forget that his main function is to glorify the Son, so that if our life is not always pointing to the Lord Jesus Christ and glorifying him, we had better be careful. There are other spirits, and these other spirits are very powerful, and can give wonderful gifts. Satan can counterfeit most of the gifts of the Holy Spirit. For example, there are spirits who can heal. There are strong phenomena in this world in which we live, and the test of the gifts of the Spirit is this: do they testify to the fact that Jesus is God in the flesh? Do they glorify the Son of God? As that is the supreme work of the Holy Spirit, so every spirit must be tested by that particular test.

How, then, does the Holy Spirit glorify Christ? It seems to me that the best way to look at this is to divide it into three main headings. First of all, he reveals the Lord Jesus Christ and his person. Paul in his letter to the Corinthians talks about the Lord of glory. Paul writes: 'But we speak the wisdom of God in a mystery . . . which none of the princes of this world knew: for had they known it, they would not have crucified the Lord of glory' (1 Cor 2:7–8). But we, he says, have received the Spirit, and 'the Spirit searcheth all things, even the deep things of God'. Do you see what that means? When the Lord Jesus Christ was here as man, the Pharisees and the doctors of the law did not recognize him —it was they who incited the people to cry out, 'Away with him, crucify him.' The Greeks did not know him either, nor did the great philosophers, they all rejected him. They said it was nonsense and impossible that a carpenter like that should be the Son of God. And the reason why they did not know him was they had not received the Holy Spirit. Paul says in 1 Corinthians 12:3, 'No man can say that Jesus is the Lord, but by the Holy Ghost.'

Have you not often been perplexed by the fact that many able men in this modern world of ours do not believe in the deity of Jesus Christ? They say that he was only a man. They praise him, and say he is the greatest man, or teacher the world has ever known, but they do not see in him the Son of God. We should never be unhappy about that. To recognize the Lord Jesus Christ is not a matter of intellect, because the greatest brain can never come to see it and believe it. It is a spiritual truth and something which is spiritually discerned.

The Bible tells us that it was not surprising that these people did not believe on the Lord Jesus Christ as the Son of God. It was because they were blind, because their understanding had not been enlightened by the Holy Spirit and, in a sense, their unbelief proves the truth of the gospel. Thank God that it is not a matter of intellect, because if the recognition of the person of the Lord Jesus Christ were a matter of intellect and ability, then the way of salvation would not be a fair one. People with brains would have a great advantage over everybody else, and those who were ignorant and had not much intellectual power, would not be able to understand and grasp the truth. Consequently, they would not be saved and it would be a salvation for certain special intellectual people only.

But thank God it is not that at all! In this matter of the recognition of the Lord Jesus Christ we are all exactly on a level, we are all in the same position. The greatest brain is never big enough to understand and to grasp it, but the Holy Spirit can enable the most ignorant and the most un-intelligent to understand. A person without any educational advantages can accept the great salvation because it is the work of the Holy Spirit. The Holy Spirit alone can reveal the person of Christ, but he *can* do it and he can do it to anybody and to everybody.

Furthermore, the Holy Spirit not only reveals the person, he also reveals the work. The preaching of Christ, says Paul, is a stumbling block to the Jews, and foolishness to the Greeks (1 Cor 1:23). These so-called wise men frequently stumble at the cross especially. You see, the preaching of the first disciples was not only that Jesus of Nazareth is the Son of God, but that he came into the world in order to deal with the problem of sin. They taught that the meaning of his death upon the cross was not merely that he was arrested by the Romans at the instigation of the Pharisees, and put to death by crucifixion. No, they taught also that God had made him to be sin for us—it was a great transaction

between the Father and the Son. To the philosophers, this
was nonsense. They did not understand because they did not
receive the Holy Spirit. 'But we,' says Paul again to the
Corinthians, 'have received, not the spirit of the world, but
the Spirit which is of God; that we might know the things
that are freely given to us of God' (1 Cor 2:12).

I want to ask a simple and plain question here: have you
understood this matter of the atonement? Are you clear
about the work of Christ? Do you see and know that the
Lord Jesus Christ has taken your sins upon himself and has
died for them on the tree: Is that real to you? Does that make
sense to you, or are you stumbling at it? If you are in
difficulty, it is because you have not been enlightened by the
Holy Spirit, and, believe me, the only way you can come to
know, is not to try to understand it intellectually, but to ask
God to enlighten you by the Spirit and to enable you to see
and understand and receive this truth as he unfolds and displays the work of Christ. If you read the sermon, delivered
by Peter on the Day of Pentecost you will find him doing
that very thing.

Then the Holy Spirit not only reveals the person and work
of Christ, he also reveals the teaching of Christ. Our Lord
said to these disciples before he left them, 'I have yet many
things to say unto you, but ye cannot bear them now. How-
beit when he, the Spirit of truth, is come, he will guide you
into all truth' (Jn 16:12–13). He will remind you of the things
I have said and which you cannot grasp now and he will
make them plain to you.

So if you are in trouble about the understanding of this
gospel, ask God to give you his Spirit in all his fullness, and
you will begin to understand. The fatal thing in these matters
is to bring your natural intellect to bear upon them: 'The
natural man receiveth not the things of the Spirit of God . . .
neither can he know them, because they are spiritually discerned' (1 Cor 2:14).

Read 1 Corinthians 2 again, and understand that these

things are in a different realm, they belong to a different order, and the only way to understand the teaching of the New Testament about Christ's personal work and his teaching is to have the eyes of your understanding enlightened by the Holy Spirit. Therefore, if you are in trouble, do not waste your time trying to read books of philosophy about these matters, do not try to grasp them with the natural intellect, for it is impossible. We are dealing with miracles. We are in the realm of the supernatural and the spiritual, and the only hope for us is that the Holy Spirit will come with that unction, with his eye salve, to anoint our eyes so that they will be opened to the blessed truth.

But the Holy Spirit not only reveals Christ, he also *applies* his word, which is to convict us of sin. I have sometimes met people who have said to me, 'I do not understand this teaching about sin, I do not feel I am a sinner.' Well, if you do not feel you are a sinner, it is simply because you do not know yourself, and you do not know yourself because the Holy Spirit has not convicted you. Some of the best people who have ever trodden this earth have been those who have been most conscious of their sinfulness. I cannot imagine a worse state for anybody to be in than for him or her to say they do not feel they are sinners. The Holy Spirit convicts and convinces of sin, and if he has not done it for you, as you value your own soul, ask him to do it. Christ came to die for sinners, not for the righteous, and the first work of the Spirit is to convict of sin, of righteousness and of judgement. We come to Christ for salvation after the Spirit has convinced us of sin, because the Lord Jesus Christ is the answer to our need.

The Holy Spirit then gives us assurance of our acceptance and of our forgiveness. He is a seal given to us to show that we belong to God. He testifies with our spirits that we are the children of God. No Christian has a right to be uncertain about his or her salvation; the Holy Spirit has been given in order that we might be certain for, 'The Spirit itself beareth

witness with our spirit, that we are the children of God'
(Rom 8:16). If any Christian who is reading this is uncertain,
or is lacking in assurance and in happiness, let me urge this
upon you—ask for the gift of the Spirit in his fullness, ask for
this blessed assurance, tell God you long for it, do not give
yourself rest or peace, and, in a sense, do not give God rest
or peace until you have it. You are meant to have it, therefore pray that the Spirit will lead you to it and, if you are
genuine and sincere, you will have it. You may have been
praying for months, or even years, but go on, I say, keep his
commandments, live the life he has marked out for you, but
above all ask that the Spirit may give this witness within
you. He was sent to do that and thus he links us to Christ. It
is beyond understanding; it is the mystical union between the
believer and Christ. As our Lord said in John 15, we are
bound to Christ as the branches to the vine; his life is in us
and it is a part of this blessed work of the Spirit. Then he
goes on to work in us, sanctifying and perfecting us—'Work
out your own salvation,' says Paul in Philippians 2, 'with
fear and trembling. For it is God which worketh in you both
to will and to do of his good pleasure.' He even helps us in
our prayers: 'We know not what we should pray for as we
ought: but the Spirit itself maketh intercession for us with
groanings which cannot be uttered' (Rom 8:26). He then
goes on to produce the fruit of the Spirit in us: 'love, joy,
peace, longsuffering, gentleness, goodness, faith, meekness,
temperance' (Gal 5:22–23).

These are the things which are the work of the Spirit and
they can be summarized like this: he is sent to make the Lord
Jesus Christ real to us. So do not waste your time in trying to
picture the Lord Jesus Christ. Do not go and look at portraits
of him which are wholly imaginary. There is a sense, I believe, in which nobody should ever try to paint him—it is
wrong. I do not like these paintings of Christ, they are the
efforts of the natural mind. No, if you want a photograph of
the Lord Jesus Christ, the Holy Spirit will give it to you in

the inner man. Christ said himself, in John 14: 'He that hath my commandments, and keepeth them, he it is that loveth me: and he that loveth me shall be loved of my Father, and I will love him, and will manifest myself to him.' That is the work of the Spirit, to make Christ living, to make us certain he is there, so that when we speak to him, and he to us, the Spirit makes him real, he is formed in us. Indeed, the Spirit takes the place of the Lord Jesus Christ with us. Christ has said, 'I will not leave you comfortless.' I am going away and you are beginning to be unhappy, but I will not leave you orphans. I will send another Comforter, the Holy Spirit. He will be with you, and he will always be with you so that you will always know what you should do. He will work in you, and you will know that you are walking with him. The Christian life is fellowship with the Father and the Son Jesus Christ, through the Holy Spirit.

And, finally, what he does is to enable us, to give us his wonderful power in order that we may witness to the Lord Jesus Christ. Have you ever thought of that? Have you ever thought about how the Christian church came into being, or how she has persisted throughout the centuries?

Have you ever thought of how that handful of ignorant men, fishermen and ordinary people, were able to turn that ancient world upside down? Have you ever wondered how it happened? There is only one answer, and that is that the power of the Holy Spirit came upon them on the Day of Pentecost. They were not able to reason or argue, it was not their eloquence or persuasive power. No, it was the mighty power of the Holy Spirit upon them!

And Paul writes the same thing about himself. He tells the Corinthians that when he preached the gospel to them at Corinth he deliberately eschewed the methods and manners of the Greek philosophers, 'For,' he says, 'I determined not to know anything among you, save Jesus Christ, and him crucified . . . and my speech and my preaching was not with enticing words of man's wisdom'—he would have nothing to do with these intellectual things—'but in demonstration of the Spirit and of power,' so that the glory might be to God and not to man (1 Cor 2:2,4).

The Holy Spirit gives this power, and, thank God, he not only gave it to the first apostles, he has also given it to quite unknown people, throughout the centuries. He has enabled some simple people just to speak the right word at the right moment. John Bunyan tells us in his autobiography, *Grace Abounding*, that one of the greatest blessings and helps he ever had was one afternoon listening to three ignorant women who were doing some knitting together in the sunshine, outside a house, and talking about the Lord Jesus Christ. He got more from them than from anybody else. And you find that that is what happens. God gives this power to the simplest, humblest Christian to testify to the Lord Jesus Christ, of what he has done and the difference he has made to human life. That is how the Holy Spirit glorifies the Son. When he works in us, what he does is to make us glorify the Lord Jesus Christ. The man in whom the Spirit dwells does not talk about himself; whether he is a preacher or whatever he may be, you do not come away talking about him.

You and I have the inestimable privilege of being men and women who in this life and in our daily work and vocation can be glorifying the Lord Jesus Christ. Oh, God grant that we all may be filled with this Spirit, the Holy Spirit, of God, that we may 'know him, and the power of his resurrection, and the fellowship of his sufferings, being made conformable unto his death'; that we may know what he has done for us; that we may know we are the children of God and joint heirs with Christ; that we may have glimpses of the glory that awaits us and that we may find our lives transformed and filled with his power, so that we may say with Paul, 'I live; yet not I, but Christ liveth in me.'

7

It Is Finished

John 17:1–5

Having considered in general the particular glory of the Father, the Son and the Holy Spirit, we come now to the place where we must look a little more closely at one of the detailed statements which are made here in these five verses. We shall be considering especially the statement in the fourth verse, where our Lord, speaking to his Father, says, 'I have glorified thee on the earth: I have finished the work which thou gavest me to do.' The two parts of that statement, of course, are complementary. He had glorified his Father on the earth by finishing the work which the Father had given him to do. He came in order to glorify the Father, and all he did accorded with this, so we can concentrate in particular on the second statement, 'I have finished the work which thou gavest me to do.' Let us therefore, look at this work about which he speaks.

It is of course one of the best ways of considering the Christian salvation; it is a glorious statement of what it all is, and of what it all involved and what it all cost. It is the way in which the Scripture constantly urges us to think about these things. Again, let me point out in passing that there is nothing that is so calculated to help us as to have a correct and large objective view of the way of salvation. It is always true that the direct road to peace, and joy and happiness, is

never to start with, and concentrate upon, yourself. It is, as
we have seen, to look, instead, at this great way of salvation,
this amazing plan; and the people who are always at peace in
this life and world are those who, to use the phrase of the
hymn writer, are 'lost in wonder, love and praise'. The hap-
piest people the world has ever known have always been
those who have had the glorious view of salvation, and who
have seen that they are 'in him'—that is the great New
Testament phrase, 'in Christ'—and that they are lost in him.
And so they live as more than conquerors in this world and
are immune to most of the things that are finally responsible
for all our unhappinesses and our miseries.

So, then, we are going to look at salvation in terms of this
comprehensive statement, 'I have finished the work which
thou gavest me to do.' Let us try to approach it in this way.
The first thing we must notice is that this work which was
given him to do is obviously something definite and special
and concrete. There is nothing vague and indefinite about
the New Testament teaching concerning Christian salvation.
It is exactly, if one may use such a term, like someone who
has been briefed to do a particular work. Now this word
'briefed' has become extended in its meaning in the last few
years. We used to think of it in terms of barristers, but we
became familiar with it during the war when men in the Air
Force were 'briefed' to do a particular thing. The work is as
definite, as concrete and as circumscribed as that; and that is
the first thought which we must always hold very clearly in
our minds with regard to this Christian salvation.

It is not a bad thing, therefore, as we begin to think about
it, to test ourselves. If someone came to me and asked me
what Christian salvation is, would I be able to give an *exact*
definition? According to this term, I should be. It is not some
general inference, or vague impression, nor is it one of those
things about which you can make a number of statements,
and yet never quite describe it. No, it is a definite and particular work, and there are, of course, many definite state-

ments with regard to what it is in the Scriptures themselves. The work that was given our Lord to do was that of saving mankind. You remember his own words: 'The Son of man is come'—why?—because he has been given a particular assignment from the Father—'to seek and to save that which was lost' (Lk 19:10).

Then look at the way in which the apostle Paul puts it in Galatians 4: 'When the fullness of the time was come, God sent forth his Son, made of a woman, made under the law, to redeem them that were under the law'—that is the particular task for which he was briefed. Or, if you like it in a more general form, we can look at it like this: the work that our Lord was given to do was the work of restoring men to fellowship and communion with God. That is exactly why he came; he came all the way from heaven to earth, and did everything he did, in order that men and women like ourselves, who were out of relationship with God, might be restored to that relationship. He came to bring together man and God. He says here, 'I have finished the work which thou gavest me to do,' and in these words he says he has given eternal life to as many as God has given him. The work is as definite as that: to reconcile men to God, to bring God and man into this particular relationship and fellowship with one another that had been lost and destroyed.

That leads me then to a second statement, which I put in this form: what was it that made this work necessary? If it had not been necessary the eternal Council would never have been held, God the Father would never have sent forth his Son into the world, and the Son would never have endured and suffered all that he did. So we see that there was some special and peculiar reason why this work was necessary. I emphasize this because I find there are so many people who never seem to have seen the necessity of this work. They say, 'I have always believed in God, and in the love of God.' But the whole of this work which Christ came to do is to them absolutely unnecessary. You ask them what they hope for

and they say that they hope they will get to heaven. If you
ask them how they are going to do so, they reply, 'Well, I
have always believed in God,' and they talk about this and
that, but they never mention the Lord Jesus Christ and his
work at all. His work is unnecessary as far as they are concerned.

Yet, obviously, by definition, this is a work which was
absolutely essential. The Son was sent, and given this assignment, because without this work man and God cannot be
reconciled. And so here, you see, we are plunged immediately into the profundities of Christian theology. What made
this work necessary was the problem raised by sin. You do
not begin to understand the work that was given to the Lord
Jesus Christ unless you are perfectly clear about the problem
of sin. Of course, we now begin to understand why it is that
there is so little said today about the plan of salvation, and
why men and women think so infrequently about this mag-
nificent scheme. It is because they do not like the doctrine of
sin and dismiss it lightly, yet that, according to the Bible, is
what made all this work necessary.

Have you ever wondered why the ceremonial regulations
were given to the Children of Israel? I mean the ceremonial
regulations about the burnt offerings and the sin offerings
and the trespass offerings—all that long list of things that had
to be done: the killing of animals, the shedding of blood and
the presenting of it in the Temple. The reason for it all is the
problem of sin and what made this work of Christ so essential was sin, and man's condition in sin.

But that was not the only thing that made it necessary.
There is something else which made it still more necessary
and that is none other than the holy character of God himself. I have to put sin first because unless I do so we cannot
see the problem that was, in a sense, raised even in the heart
of the Eternal himself. For before God and man could be
reconciled, something had got to be done both from the
standpoint of God and of man. The problem from the

Godward side I can put in this way—I use the terms used by the apostle Paul in Romans 3—how could God at one and the same time remain just and yet be the justifier of the ungodly? How could God remain holy, and unchangeable, and eternal, and righteous, true and just, and yet forgive sin and forgive the transgressions of man?

Let me put it in a simpler way. God, being God, cannot just forgive sin. Now the common idea about God, the one that we have instinctively, is that when we admit that we have sinned, all that is necessary is that we should come to God, say we are very sorry, and God will forgive us. But according to the Bible that is impossible, and I do not hesitate to use that word. As a preacher of the Christian gospel, I am compelled to say this and I say it with reverence: God, because he is God, cannot just forgive sin like that.

If you want me to prove what I am saying, this is how I do it. If God could have forgiven sin just by saying, 'I forgive', he would have done so, and Christ would never have been sent into this world. The work that was given to him to do, this work, this assignment, this task, was given to the Lord Jesus Christ because, I say again, without it, God cannot forgive sin. He must not only justify the ungodly, he must remain just. The way of salvation must be consistent with the character of God. He cannot deny himself, he cannot change himself, he is unchangeable. 'God is light, and in him is no darkness at all'; (1 Jn 1:5); he is 'the Father of lights, with whom is no variableness, neither shadow of turning' (Jas 1:17). He is eternally, everlastingly, the same, and he is absolutely righteous and holy and just. He cannot remain that and simply forgive sin and no more.

So you see this work of Christ was absolutely essential and I think we can see why it is that many people's ideas of salvation are so terribly wrong. They really do not see the necessity for Christ himself and his work; they say, 'God is love and because he is love, he will forgive me.' My friend, he cannot, because he *is* God! The work of Christ was essential because of the character of God, and it was essential because of man in sin; something had to be done to render man fit for God. So there are two mighty reasons why this work was essential.

Let us go on to another problem. The work was something that Christ himself had to do, and he can therefore speak of it as being done. 'I have finished the work which thou gavest me to do.' Now I want to put that in the form of a negative like this. The Lord Jesus Christ did not come into this world to tell us what *we* have to do. He came himself to do something for us which we could never do for ourselves. These negatives are all so essential, because there are people who believe in the deity of the Lord Jesus Christ, but if you ask them what he came into this world to do, their answer will be that he came to tell us what we must do ourselves. Or they talk about good works and say that if we do this or that we will make ourselves Christian and make ourselves right with God. No! Our Lord says here, '*I* have finished the work which thou gavest *me* to do.'

I am sometimes afraid that we are all guilty of missing the wood because of the trees, and sometimes the people who are most guilty are those who delight to call themselves Bible students. They go through the gospels with their analyses and look at the Lord's teaching, but they are so taken up with the details that they never see the whole grand plan itself. The truth which we have to take hold of is that which is emphasized here, and the best way to understand it is to consider what it was that he did, and, too, what he was doing beforehand. He came to do certain things himself, and we are saved by what Christ has done for us, and not by what he tells us to do. The work of salvation is his work and his doing, and he came specifically to do it, and here, in these words, he looks ahead, as it were, to the death on the cross, as well as back to what he has already done. Under the shadow of the cross, he reviews the whole work, and he is able to say, 'I have finished the work which thou gavest me to do.' I have completed it. On the cross he said it again in the words, 'It is finished.' It is his work and not yours and mine. So a very good way of testing whether we have a right or wrong way of looking at salvation is to ask ourselves whether we see Christian salvation as something which is exclusively and entirely the work of the Lord Jesus Christ. We are his workmanship; it is all of God in Christ. He has completed the work, and we simply have to receive his salvation as a free gift.

That leads me to what is, of course, the most important thing of all, which is to look in detail at something of this work which he has done. Here again I want to emphasize that the work which Christ came to do was not simply to give us incomparable teaching about God, and about the love and the fatherhood of God. How often has that been put forward as the sole business of Christ in this world? He did that, of course, but that is not the specific purpose for which he came. That had already been revealed in the Old Testament. In the Old Testament you have some of the most glorious statements of the character and love of God, and of the fatherhood of God; you will find statements there that are in no sense inferior to the statements of the New Testament. God's ancient people had been taught about him in his love, and in his fatherhood, and in his holy character; they knew them, in a sense, and Christ did not come only to tell us those things.

Or look at it like this. Whatever else Christ came to do, we must realize that it was something that necessitated the incarnation, the life, the death and the resurrection of the Son of God. So when I come to face this question of what this work was, I must be certain that my answer defines it in a way that makes the incarnation an absolute necessity, the death on the cross an absolute necessity, and the resurrection an absolute necessity. The teaching concerning the love and character and fatherhood of God, therefore, has to make the fact of these great truths inevitable.

But the same thing is true with regard to our teaching about his death upon the cross, we must so define the work, and all these events, as to make them absolute necessities. And the way to approach them is to understand that the problem was about how God and man could be reconciled. It was not merely that man might know certain things about God. Something had to be done to bring them into fellowship and communion with one another. If we remember that *that* is the controlling thought, I think we will begin to see exactly what the work was which the Lord was sent to do. He is the One who was sent in order to bring that to pass; he is the One who has come as the Messiah; he has come to seek and to save, to be the Mediator, between God and man.

'The work', in other words, is that he was appointed as man's representative. Man at the beginning had a representative called Adam. He was the entire human race in himself, and acted as its representative, so that when he sinned, we all sinned. What is the answer to this? It is that we need someone to represent us with God, someone who alone can lift us up again, someone who can set us free, and present and introduce us to God. That is the task and nothing less than that. What was necessary was a representative of mankind, or, to use the phrase in Hebrews 2, we need 'a captain of our salvation', a leader, someone who can speak for us. A new originator of a new race, corresponding to Adam, was essential, and it was in order to do this that the Son of God came into this world, and the special task that was given to him involved this.

First of all, of course, it involved the incarnation. A new humanity is necessary, a new man, if you like, who can stand before God on our behalf, and the Son of God came in order to start this new humanity. That is why he ever came into the world, that is why the miracle of the virgin birth ever took place, and that is why you have the mystery and the marvel of the God-Man—two natures in the one person. That is why, as Hebrews 2 puts it, he held out a helping hand

and took on himself the seed of Abraham. He took humanity into his deity: that is the whole meaning of the incarnation, that is precisely what happened at Bethlehem. So the point I am emphasizing is that his task was not merely to tell us about God and his love. He could have done that in the form of a theophany—he could have made one of those appearances to mankind, and given certain revelations about God and his love. But that is not enough: he has to represent man, and he became man, hence the incaration. Before he can represent us as High Priest he has to become one of us, so he takes unto himself human nature.

But it means even more than that, for having been born as man, in the likeness of sinful flesh, he then went to John the Baptist and asked John to baptize him. John stood back in amazement and said, 'I have need to be baptized of thee, and comest thou to me?'

No, said Christ, 'Suffer it to be so now: for thus it becometh us to fulfil all righteousness.'

What was happening there at that baptism? It is, again, one of those essential steps in this great work that he came to do. Being born a man was not enough in and of itself, he had to do this as well. He was absolutely sinless, why then did he need to be baptized? He was baptized because he identified himself with us in our sin. He was taking the responsibility for us and our sins, and taking our sinfulness upon himself.

Or you can look at it in another way: it was at his baptism that the Holy Spirit came upon him in the form of a dove, which means that not only was he being given strength, he was being anointed for his task. He was being set aside in a very special way as the Messiah, the Anointed One who was to deliver the people for whom he had come. Therefore, he had his ordination, the oil of the Spirit was poured upon him, and he was announced as the Messiah. So the baptism was essential; it was part of the work which he came to do, which was not only to take on our nature but to identify himself with us in sin.

Then we can go on and watch him and see his life of
perfect, spotless obedience. Once again, he did not live a
perfect life simply in order to show that he was the Son of
God. No, something much more profound, and much more
vital for you and for me, had to take place. It was that in
living that perfect life of obedience to the law he was not
only honouring the law as our head and representative, but
also as the captain of our salvation, as the first born among
many brethren. He was honouring the law for you and for
me and for all who believe in him; he was not only gaining
positive righteousness for himself, he was gaining it for us.
He was keeping God's law for us and it was part of the work
he came to do.

Is it not true to say that far too often we tend, as we read
the gospel, to admire his perfect life and say, 'Yes, he is
undoubtedly God as well as man', and then to stop at that?
But we should always look at him and see him honouring
God's law and keeping it perfectly, and we should see that
he was doing it as your representative and mine. He was
doing it for us: he came to do that, not merely to teach about
God and the forgiveness and love of God. He had to honour
God's law before God could forgive us, and he did that.

But not only that, we behold him conquering Satan. In
Hebrews 2, which is a great commentary upon this very
verse we are considering together, we are told that he came
into the world that 'through death he might destroy him that
had the power of death, that is, the devil; and deliver them
who through fear of death were all their lifetime subject to
bondage' (Heb 2:14–15). John in his first epistle says that
Jesus came into the world to destroy the works of the devil.
In other words, mankind in sin had become subject to Satan,
and before we could be saved, and before we could be truly
reconciled to God, Satan had to be conquered. We had to be
emancipated and delivered out of the dominion of Satan and
transferred to the kingdom of God, and it is only Christ who

could do that. All who came before him and who tried to be
emancipated from the thraldom of Satan, had been defeated
and overcome by the devil. So before we could be redeemed
the devil had to be conquered. Our Lord had to do it, and he
had to do it as a man, before our freedom could take place—
and he has done it.

And then, of course, he was confronted by the final task,
which was to deliver us from the guilt of sin, and that is the
whole meaning of his death upon the cross. There I see him
allowing sin to be punished in his body and giving himself as
a sin offering, for without the shedding of blood, there is no
remission of sin (see Hebrews 9:22). That is true of God.
God, because he is what he is, cannot forgive us sinners
without the shedding of blood. Before God could forgive
sin, it had to be punished, and by Christ's death upon the
cross your sins and mine have been dealt with. They have
been punished, their guilt has been expiated—there on the
cross he was made sin for us, 'God was in Christ reconciling
the world unto himself' (2 Cor 5:19). So Christ has come to
do this—this work of presenting himself as a man without
spot and without blemish, and it could not have been done
without his coming into this world and without his doing all
he did. And so, by doing this, he has conquered death as
well. He has taken the sting out of it because 'the sting of
death is sin; and the strength of sin is the law. But thanks be
to God, which giveth us the victory through our Lord Jesus
Christ' (1 Cor 15:56–57).

I merely put these headings before you. I plead with you
to consider them one by one at your leisure. That was the
work which he came to do. He came in order to honour
God's law perfectly by keeping it, by living it. He came to
satisfy it by bearing the punishment he pronounced upon sin
and guilt and evil. He has done that, and thus the law is
satisfied. Yes, but as I have reminded you, we need to be
delivered from the power of the devil, we need death and the
grave to be conquered, and he has done it all. And beyond all

that, we need a new nature, because we need not only forgiveness of sins, but to be made fit to have communion and
fellowship with God. We need to have a nature that can
stand the sight of God, for 'God is light and in him is no
darkness at all'. And Christ has come and given us himself,
his own nature, the eternal life of which he speaks in this
very prayer that we are considering together.

So here, looking at it all, he can say, 'I have finished the
work which thou gavest me to do.' He has done everything
that is necessary for man to be reconciled to God. Have you
realized, my friends, that this work is finished? Have you
realized that it is finished as far as you are concerned? Do you
still think that you have to make yourself a Christian? You
are asked whether you are a Christian, and you reply that
you are hoping to be, but that you need to do this, that and
that other . . . No! Christ says, 'I have finished the work
which thou gavest me to do.' The work has been done, and
what proves whether we are truly Christians or not is the
fact that we know and realize that the work has been done,
and that we rest, and rest only, upon the finished work of
our blessed Lord and Saviour Jesus Christ. If we see it all in
him and the work done and completed in him, it means we
are Christian; if in any sense we are uncertain or doubtful, or
think we have to do something ourselves, it means we are
not. The beginning of Christianity is the acceptance of this
statement: 'I have finished the work which thou gavest me to
do.' The way for you to know God, and to be reconciled to
him, is wide open in the Lord Jesus Christ, and his perfect
work on your behalf. If you have never entered in before,
enter in now, rest upon the finished work of the Lord Jesus
Christ and begin to rejoice, immediately, in your great salvation.

8

The Hour Is Come

John 17:1

I want in particular now to look at the phrase, 'the hour is come'. My whole case is that if we fail or falter in the Christian life, either in thought or in action, if we are unhappy or defeated, if in any way we are failing to function in this world as a Christian should, and as the Christian life is portrayed so plainly in the New Testament, then such failure is ultimately due to the fact that our view of our position as Christian people in Christ Jesus is in some way or another defective.

There is no question but that the New Testament has the answer to all the problems and difficulties of the Christian life, and its object is to bring us back to the truth itself and to give us a still clearer view of it. So we are not doing something theoretical. There is nothing more fatal than the kind of dichotomy that some people seem to recognize between belief and life, faith and practice, for these are indissolubly mixed. The most practical people, who pride themselves on being so, the people who say they are not very interested in doctrine, but who believe in *doing* things, are the very people who will, sooner or later, find themselves in grave trouble. It is fatal only to recognize one or the other—the two things must be taken together. So we have spent some time in looking at this plan of salvation as it is unfolded here.

But now we must look at this phrase, 'Father, the hour is
come', for the great doctrine concerning 'this hour' is again
something that is of vital importance to us. In a sense, the
whole of salvation is seen as we look at our Lord facing this
hour, and the very essence of the truth is emphasized by the
doctrine that is here outlined. As he points out so often, he
came from heaven, and did all that we were considering
earlier in order to come to this hour, for this hour was essential to the completion of that work which the Father had
given him to do. There can be no doubt but that this hour is
the focus and climax, at one and the same time, of everything that our Lord came to do. It is the crucial, climactic
point in the whole of that mighty work that we have been
looking at in general.

The best way, it seems to me, of approaching the teaching
and doctrine concerning 'this hour' is that we should remind
ourselves of some of the statements which our Lord himself
made with respect to it. For instance, we are told that on the
occasion of the marriage in Cana of Galilee, when his mother
asked him to do something about the shortage of wine, he
turned to her and said, 'Woman, what have I to do with
thee? mine hour is not yet come' (Jn 2:4). He is already
speaking of it. Again, he had to say the same thing to his
brethren who upbraided him for not going to the feast at
Jerusalem. He said, 'My time is not yet come' (Jn 7:6), and
that phrase has a special meaning to it. Then we are told on
another occasion that his enemies sought to take him, but
that, 'No man laid hands on him, because his hour was not
yet come' (Jn 7:30). Later on we read again that no man laid
hands on him for his hour was not yet come (Jn 8:20).

Then take the statement in John 12:23, 'And Jesus
answered them, saying, The hour is come, that the Son of
man should be glorified.' And, just after that, hear him saying, 'Now is my soul troubled; and what shall I say? Father,
save me from this hour: but for this cause came I unto this
hour.' Then there is the reference in the thirteenth chapter to

the same thing: 'When Jesus knew that his hour was come
. . .' and again, later, he says, 'Behold the hour cometh, yea,
is now come, that ye shall be scattered, every man to his
own, and shall leave me alone.' Then we have the statement
here, 'Father, the hour is come. . .' and there is also another
very interesting and important statement in Luke 22:53,
where we read that he turned to the authorities that were
against him and hated him and said, '. . .but this is your
hour, and the power of darkness.'

Now in order to interpret this verse in John 17 aright, we
must bear all this in mind, and as we do so, I think there are
certain things which can be said quite plainly. The first is that
this 'hour' is obviously a predetermined hour. You notice
that all those statements regarding it have something very
special, and definite to say. When he says, 'Mine hour is not
yet come', he is, in effect, telling them, 'My time is not yet
come; your time is always here, but there is a special time as
far as I am concerned. You want me to come and declare
myself; no, you do not understand it, the time for that has
not yet come.' In other words, you find our Lord always
looking forward to this hour. Indeed this theme of expec-
tation is to be found running right through the whole of
Scripture.

This whole problem of time is a particularly important
and fascinating one; there are some who would say that in
many ways it is the biggest and most important point in the
whole of theology, and the question of how to relate time, as
we know it, to eternity and timelessness causes a great deal
of confusion. Now if you are a philosopher, it can be a
profound problem, yet, if we take the Scripture as it is, I
think it becomes comparatively plain and clear. God has
brought the time process into being, and, having done so, he
has appointed that certain things should take place at a certain
time. It is not that God is bound by time, but that he has
ordered that things should happen in the realm of time, and
thus you find in the Old Testament and in the New that God

has appointed minutes.

Take the flood as an illustration. God had said, 'My Spirit shall not always strive with man' (Gen 6:3). He had focussed upon a determined point; he was able to call Noah to start building the ark 120 years before the flood came. He knew when the flood was coming—all these things are plain and open unto the eye of God. And so it was that 'when the fullness of the time was come'—when the hour had come—'God sent forth his Son, made of a woman, made under the law, to redeem them that were under the law' (Gal 4:3–4).

This, surely, is a thought that liberates us at once from most of the thraldom of life in this world. You look at life today, and at history, and at the whole course of the world, and if you look at it with the human eye alone, you will find it very difficult to see any meaning in it. But the moment we begin to look at it in the light of this doctrine of 'the hour', though we may not understand it fully with all its details, we can at once be certain that the Lord still reigns and that life in this world is not out of hand. As we read this biblical history and see the clashing of the nations, with the people opposed to God, and apparently out of control, we find that at a given point God does redeem the world in spite of man. When God's time arrives God comes in and the whole world has to conform again to his plan and purpose.

So the great consolation for us is that though we see the Christian church and Christianity derided and apparently counting for so little in this modern world; and though we may see on the surface that the enemy opposed to the church is triumphant all along the line, and that God's people are languishing, we nevertheless know for certain, beyond any doubt whatsoever, that God's hand is still upon the situation, and that in a moment he can arise and confound all his enemies. 'He that sitteth in the heavens shall laugh' (Ps 2:4), as he sees these pigmies exalting themselves, for he knows that at a word he can destroy them, and they will perish out of sight.

But in particular for our purpose as we consider the plan of salvation, the important thing is that all the things that happened to him did not take our Lord by surprise. That has been the fatal view of our Lord, his person and his work, ever since the advent of the so called higher criticism movement. They represent our Lord as a human teacher who had his plan of teaching the people, his own nation, and converting them to his point of view, and then sending them out to spread this wonderful teaching. But, suddenly, these people tell us, after three years the whole thing came crashing to the ground. He never anticipated this rejection, they say, he never thought they had it in their hearts to do such a thing. That is the picture that is painted, and we are left feeling very sorry for this 'pale Galilean', this incomparable teacher, this Galilean peasant, born before his time with his exalted idealism, and so on, who saw it all brought to nothing, and broke his heart at the failure of it all, so that he died of a broken heart upon the cross.

What a travesty of this glorious gospel! My friend, he came from heaven, he laid aside his glory, as we were considering earlier, in order to come to 'this hour'. He knew it from the beginning. He came to die, specifically to die. We have seen that, apart from that death on the cross, he cannot deliver me; that apart from the death on the cross, I say it again with reverence, even God cannot forgive man. The cross is absolutely essential, the cross was planned before the world was ever created. So the hour that produced the cross is the central, pivotal point, of history and God always knew about it, the Lord came for that hour. So we must never think of this hour as taking him by surprise, it was an hour that was appointed and determined, it was the crisis of the world itself.

But let us go on to the second point, that this hour is the crucial hour of history. There is no question about that. It was the most momentous hour since the beginning of the world, it is indeed the turning point which determines everything—it is the greatest event, the most—yes, let me use the word again—climactic event that has ever taken place in this world. Everything leads up to that hour, everything eventuates from that hour. That is the hour to which the whole of prophecy is looking forward, and to which the whole of the church, and her doctrine and history look back. It is the central, focal, point which determines and controls everything. It was the point on which everything that God had planned depended, and if there were failure at this point everything would fail. Hence our Lord's prayer to his Father, 'the hour is come glorify thy Son, that thy Son may glorify thee'.

If the Son had failed at this particular point, everything else would have been useless. His teaching would have been of no value whatsoever, because, though we might have tried to live it, and carry it out, yet we would have lacked the strength and the power. He would have been giving us a law even more impossible than the law given through Moses, and thereby he would have condemned us and left us under a still greater condemnation. It is the most vital hour of all, for, I say again, if he cannot bear the punishment of our sins, then he does not save us. But having borne the punishment, he *does* save us, so it is what happened in that hour that really holds, within itself, the entirety of our salvation.

There are people who would sometimes preach a gospel apart from this. You ask them what the gospel is, and they reply that the gospel is the Lord Jesus Christ somehow or other giving new life to men, lifting men out of their failure and giving them new life. And they sometimes present that without mentioning the cross. But, my friends, before you and I need a new life, we need forgiveness. Something has to be done about the past before we face the future. You cannot suddenly decide that you are going to live a better life, you have to deal with the problem of your past and your sin. It is this hour that deals with that, for there is no regeneration, no new life, except for those who are forgiven and justified in the sight of God. This, then, is a crucial hour.

But I must say something about what I would call the drama of the hour. There is a kind of mystery about this hour. It is very interesting as one reads the gospels to keep one's eye on the references to it. We have been looking at our Lord coming up to this hour, but he is not the only one who is preparing for it. The forces on the other side are also interested in this same hour and you can watch the plan developing from their side as well as from his side. That is where the statement in Luke 22 comes in—'this is your hour'. You cannot read the story of our Lord's experiences without seeing this tremendous fight, and I am emphasizing it here because nothing is so sad to me as the failure of many people to realize the conflict that is going on in this world. We are ready to fight against certain evil tendencies, but over and above the fight against the sin that is within us, there is this cosmic fight against sin.

There is a sense in which the Bible is nothing but a great drama in which you find depicted the mighty conflict between God and the powers of hell. The background to the Bible is something that happened before human history began—the great question of the devil and the origin of the devil and of evil. We do not know everything about it—it has not pleased God to reveal everything—but he has re-vealed this much, that quite apart from our history there was a kind of cosmic fall. As we have seen, one of the greatest of God's angelic beings rebelled against him. He is the devil, called Satan, and his one object is to defeat God. And what is unfolded in this great drama in the Bible is the attempt of the devil to destroy God's works, and to defeat God. God made his world perfect—Paradise—but the devil came in and started a fight. He persuaded man that an injustice had been done against him, and the whole of humanity, and the whole universe.

And the fight continues. Read your Bible with that in view and you will find it will be a transformed book; you will see the failure in God's own people, quite apart from the others, and it is all because the devil tried to turn them against God. You find it even when the Son of God comes into this world. The devil tried to destroy him at the beginning, the moment he was born. He took hold of King Herod and persuaded him to try to destroy this Child, this Messiah, the Saviour. Keep your eye on the malignity of the scribes and Pharisees, and the doctors of the law and the violent hatred that was manifested by them because they saw in him the representative of God. You remember how the devil said the thing explicitly on one occasion, 'I know thee who thou art; the Holy One of God' (Lk 4:34). They realized that they were fighting for their lives. The devil tempted him in the wilderness; the devil was fighting for his life and the whole of his forces were being marshalled for this ultimate clash when the two forces came together. And the clash takes place at this tremendous hour, when the Son of God is going to give his life a ransom for many. So we have to look at this hour from both these angles.

What, then, does our Lord mean exactly when he says in the Garden of Gethsemane, 'This is your hour, and the power of darkness'? It seems to me that the only possible explanation must be that this hour would never have come to pass were it not for the power of darkness. What makes this hour and all that it involves necessary and essential? It is again the problem of sin and of evil, the problem of Satan and of hell. It is the kind of hour that the devil has staged and brought into being, for, in one sense, he has manipulated it, though in a much higher sense he has not. I think that this is the way to look at it—it is the work of the devil that makes the hour essential from God's standpoint; it is because of what Satan has produced by sin and evil that God has to do this in order to overcome it.

So it is, in a sense, their hour, and it is there that we really see the essence of evil and of sin. It is such a terrible thing that nothing less than this could deal with it. It is not a question of

God's love and forgiveness, it is evil that has to be dealt with
in this radical way. The devil has produced such a situation
that this hour alone can deal with it.

So this hour can be described as 'their hour', and the hour
of the glorification of the Son at the same time, and that is
why he prays that his Father may glorify him. It is in going
through this hour, that has been produced by Satan and hell,
that our Lord really is glorified. It is there we know for
certain that he is the Son of God. No one had ever before had
to meet Satan and conquer him, no one had been able to
destroy the power that Satan had over death—that is the way
the author of the epistle to the Hebrews puts it: 'That
through death he might destroy him that had the power of
death' (2:14) and thus he sets the children free, and Christ has
done it through this, his glorification. The death and the
resurrection is the proof that he is the Son of God.

But let us, if we can, try for a moment, with reverence, to
look at it in this way. What did this hour mean to our Lord
himself? Well, he has given us an indication. Consider the
statement in John 12:27, 'Now is my soul troubled; and what
shall I say? Father, save me from this hour'—then he answers
himself and says—'but for this cause came I unto this hour.'
There I think is the right approach to any consideration of
what this hour meant to him. He knew it was coming, he
had known that all along, and now here he was actually
facing it. But although his soul was troubled, he did not ask
God, his Father, to save him from this hour. No, that was
impossible, he could not do that, for 'this hour' was his
reason for coming to the world.

'Well,' says someone, 'if he always knew about this hour,
if he had come from heaven in order to come to this hour, if
he knew for certain, as he did, that beyond that hour he was
going to rise again from the grave and go to the glory'—
indeed, every time our Lord spoke to his disciples about his
coming death, he always went on to speak of the resurrection. He knew he was going to rise again, and go to the

glory. The author of the epistle to the Hebrews reminds us
of that when he says. 'who for the joy that was set before
him endured the cross'—'so then,' the questioner continues,
'if all that is true why does he say, "now is my soul
troubled"? How could he know the glory that is coming,
and the triumph of the resurrection? How could he know he
had come to this climactic hour which was going to make
salvation possible and yet say, "Now is my soul troubled,"
and, "Father, save me from this hour"? What was the cause
of the trouble?'

There are those who think this is quite a simple problem.
They say it was nothing but his physical shrinking from
death; he knew about the glory of the resurrection, but the
thought of physical suffering troubled him and he shrank
from it as a man. In his body, in his flesh, he shrank from the
thought of this physical dissolution. But to me that very
thought is insulting. It is not only insulting to our Lord as a
man, it is such a tragic failure to understand what happened
there. No, that is no explanation, for if you accept it, then
you make our Lord a lesser person than the martyrs. The
martyrs faced death without a fear because they believed the
gospel of the resurrection. Their knowledge of it was nothing by contrast with our Lord's knowledge, but it was
enough to enable them to go boldly to the stake without a
quiver or a fear. And so that supposition makes our Lord less
than his own followers and inferior to some of his own
martyrs. No, such an explanation is impossible. It is a tragic
blindness that makes us try to view these things from the
standpoint of human reasoning, instead of in terms of
biblical doctrine.

What, then, did he shrink from? What was it that troubled
his holy, righteous soul? It was the fact that he knew what
was going to happen in that hour. He knew that the full,
total wrath of God against sin was to be manifested and
poured out against him—*that* was what he shrank from. If
physical suffering holds no terrors to a courageous man who

may not even be a Christian, it is still less to a Christian saint or martyr, and to the Son of God, it is nothing at all. There was only one thing that the Son of God shrank from, and that was to be separated from the face of his Father; he shrank from anything that could interrupt that love that had existed between them from all eternity. The one thing the Son of God shrank from was to look into his Father's face and see there that holy wrath against sin, and he knew that that was what he would have to experience in that hour. His soul was to be made an offering for sin, he himself was to be made sin, so that at that hour God was going to look at him, and he was not going to see the Son in whom he was well pleased, but this horrible, foul, ugly thing.

And that is why the Son says, in effect, 'Now is my soul troubled—what shall I say? Shall I ask him to save me from this hour? No, because if I do, I shall not save man from all that wrath of God which shall be poured out upon me. I have come for that hour, it is the purpose of my coming into this world. God cannot be just and the justifier of the ungodly unless I bear it, so I will bear it.' 'That hour'—his hour—what an hour!

The one thing, therefore, that made him speak like this was his certain clear knowledge of what was involved in this one moment, as it were, and it was the thing that broke his heart. It was the thing that killed him. In a sense, our Lord did not die of crucifixion, but because the wrath of God against sin was so poured out upon him. We are told that the soldiers, when they came, were amazed that he was dead already. Crucifixion was a slow process of death, the man who was crucified took a long time to die, but here was one who died quickly, and they were amazed. And the cause of it was a ruptured heart. So that is why his soul was troubled. It was the thought of losing the face of his Father, the thing that made him cry out on the cross. 'My God, my God, why hast thou forsaken me?' He really saw sin, and he was made sin, and all God's holy wrath against him was poured on him. He bore it all and that is what the hour meant to him.

But I want to say a final word on the results of the hour, which are put very plainly by Jesus in John 12:31. What an hour this is! Do you not begin to see that it is the most momentous hour of all time? We talk about those pivotal points of history, but they are all nothing when you look at this. 'Now is the judgement of this world'—the whole world, in the sense that it is the hour in which the world was really revealed for what it is. It was there that sin was revealed. There, shown plainly and clearly once and for ever, is the whole state of mankind apart from God. I do not know whether we realize this as we ought; sin is something so fiendish and so foul that it led to that terrible hour. So the next time the devil tempts you, remember that you will not merely be doing something which you should not be doing. No, you will be putting yourself into the realm of sin, opposed to God. But not only does the cross reveal sin for what it is, at one and the same time it pronounces doom on the whole world and everything that belongs to that realm. The cross of Jesus Christ makes this great proclamation. Unless I believe in him, unless I believe that his death at that hour is the only thing that reconciles me to God, I remain under the wrath of God. If I do not see that the wrath of God against my sin has been borne there by the Son of God, then the alternative is that I must live to experience the wrath of God: that is the essence of the Christian gospel. I either believe that my sins have been punished in the body of the Son of God or else they will be punished in me. It is the judgement of the world.

The world apart from him is under the wrath of God, it is doomed, it is damned and he alone can save it in that way. There was no other way, for God would never have allowed his Son to endure all that if there had been another way. It is the only way, so it is the judgement of the world. And we, all of us, either believe that the Lord Jesus Christ saved us in that hour, or else we remain in our sins, we belong to the

world that is going to be condemned and finally judged. The
gospel tells us that he will come back again and that this time
he will return to judge. The one question that will face
everybody is this: do you belong to him or do you not? The
books will be opened; the names of the people who believe
in Christ are in one book, the book of the Lamb of God, and
if you belong to his book you are saved. But the world is
damned and destroyed and cast into a lake of fire—the judgement of this world. But the judgement was pronounced at
the cross. Though the *nature* has been postponed and is still
being postponed, judgement has been pronounced, so that
anyone who dies without believing on the Lord Jesus Christ
belongs to the world and that has already had judgement
pronounced upon it.

Likewise, the prince of this world shall be cast out. The
devil has already been defeated, for Christ defeated him on
the cross. The devil was working up to this hour, and when
the Lord died he thought he had defeated him at last, but he
did not realize the truth of the resurrection. Christ rose again
and by so doing he has destroyed principalities and powers
and triumphed over them by his own cross, which they
thought was their masterpiece. The very death which they
thought was his defeat turns out to be the greatest victory of
all and by it they are finally doomed. The devil is still very
active in this world, but he is already defeated. In a sense he is
already cast out, and has no authority at all. Christ's people,
all who belong to Christ, all that the Father has given him,
are going to be drawn to him. The devil is already defeated,
and is going to be cast into that lake of fire and will be
destroyed eternally.

What an hour! Oh, that the Holy Spirit would open our
eyes to see and to know something of these things! We are
talking about historical events, this hour belongs to time, it
belongs to history. It is not an idea, it is not some wonderful
theory that men have woven out of their imagination. These
things have literally happened, so I am left with this fact that

the Son of God has been in this world, and has passed
through that hour for my sins. If I believe that, I know that
that hour is the one which has saved me from everlasting
destruction, but if I do not believe, I am left condemned.
Our Lord puts it again in John 12: 'I came not to judge the
world . . . the word that I have spoken, the same will
judge. . .' (verses 47,48). Though he did not come to judge,
yet he is giving his judgement. We cannot escape, the devil is
judged by this hour, the world is judged by this hour.

Oh, may God grant us to see sin for what it really is! We
cannot be indifferent to these things, for if we believe them
our way of life is going to be determined. If I believe all this,
how can I be indifferent to sin? No, the One who has done
this for me deserves my life, my soul, my all. He must be
my Lord and my Master. I say again that failure in the
Christian life is the failure really to see the meaning of this
hour, to see the meaning of sin, the failure to realize what he
suffered for you, the failure to realize the consequences of not
believing in him. May God give us grace, therefore, to meditate upon this hour, this astounding, crucial, climactic hour
in which the essence of our salvation was worked out and
achieved by the Son of God in his terrible agony and suffering upon the cross.

9

'That He Should Give Eternal Life to as Many as Thou Hast Given Him'

John 17:2

No one, I think, reading the New Testament, can fail to see that it is the most lyrical document. The great note that runs right through it all, in spite of the tragic things that it has to record, is the note of victory, and rejoicing. You find it in the gospels, and in the Acts of the Apostles, and you find it in the epistles. Our Lord himself, right under the shadow of the cross, spent a good deal of his time showing his followers how, in spite of the things that are about to happen to him, they could nevertheless be full of rejoicing. He has a joy to give them, he tells them, that no man can ever take from them. Temporarily, they will be cast down because of his crucifixion, but soon they are going to receive that joy which the world cannot understand and can never take away, and certainly the Acts of the Apostles is one of the most exhilarating books that has ever been written. In spite of everything those first Christians stood out, dominating the whole world, full of joy and rejoicing, and the great appeal in all the epistles in that those Christians to whom they were written, should rejoice. That is the great characteristic note of the New Testament, and the same thing has been true of all the great hymns of the church throughout the centuries.

> Children of the heavenly King,
> As ye journey sweetly sing,

says John Cennick, and as these men have contemplated their salvation in every century and every country it has been something that has always led them to 'wonder, love and praise'. The note of praise is dominant and characteristic, and, therefore, this is what we, who claim to be Christian, should be experiencing. A miserable Christian is, in a sense, a contradiction in terms. A Christian is one who is meant to be rejoicing, full of a sense of wonder, of praise and of adoration as he contemplates this great salvation. Furthermore, he rejoices in spite of his circumstances, for the gospel of Jesus Christ, thank God, not only offers to make us happy when all is going well with us, its great aim is that we should be able to rejoice even in tribulation and in the worst circumstances. That is its plan, and this is something that we all ought to be experiencing. But, it we are honest and frank, I think that many of us would have to admit that that is not our condition, and I am suggesting in these studies that the real explanation of that is our failure to grasp and understand the greatness of this Christian salvation.

Now, so far, we have been concentrating on it from the godward side, and we have been trying to see salvation as conceived in the mind of the eternal God, planned before the foundation of the world, and the work divided up between the Father, Son and Holy Spirit. And I would say again that if, as the result of doing all that, we are still unmoved, we are still not amazed and astounded, if we still do not feel that this is the most precious and wonderful thing in the world and that everything else in comparison with this pales into utter insignificance, then, as I understand my New Testament, it is high time we examined ourselves very seriously and discovered whether we are Christian at all. If a man can contemplate this salvation as thus looked at from the standpoint of God himself without feeling its greatness, then I do not understand such a person. Surely if one really sees these things even dimly and vaguely, it must revolutionize one's mind and it must be the dominating factor in the whole of our existence.

But now we must move on to a further aspect of the subject. I feel there is a second explanation of our failure to be rejoicing as we ought to be as Christians, and that is our failure really to grasp this salvation from *our* side, not only from God's side, but also from our own. This is surely something that should fill us with a sense of astonishment. If we read our New Testament and consider what the gospel of Jesus Christ really offers us, and then look at ourselves and our life and experience, we are confronted by this tremendous gulf. So we go on to ask the obvious question—why do we rob ourselves like this? We have all this wealth and riches offered us, why are we so poor?

Now I suggest to you that this is really the problem that confronts us all. In a worldly sense, if we were offered great wealth and riches, we would need no encouragement to take hold of them and possess them. But here we are offered the greatest riches of all, the fullness of God, the treasures of grace and wisdom that God has placed for us in the Lord Jesus Christ, the fullness that the New Testament speaks of, that is available for us, and yet we continue in a state of penury and poverty. We are half-hearted and ill at ease and shuffling along, instead of availing ourselves of these greatest of all riches. Why is it? That is the great question. Why do Christian people need these encouragements and exhortations?

And the answer is, according to the Bible, that it is all due to sin. We have a mighty enemy and adversary of our souls, one whose supreme object is not only to rob God of his glory, but to rob God's people of the things that God has provided for them. And, of course, as he robs us of the blessings, he is most effectively robbing God of his glory also, because, as far as this world is concerned, God's greatest glory is his people. God expresses his praise and glory most of all in his people, so if God's people are apologetic, hesitant, unhappy and uncertain, God is being robbed of his glory. Therefore the devil concentrates on that. The teaching of Scripture is that he is ever busy in trying to stand between us and a full realization of what God has intended for us in the Lord Jesus Christ.

He fights, he thwarts us, he dulls our faculties, he holds us down and he binds us to earth. So, as I see it, the great function of Christian preaching is not only to warn us of these things, but also, positively, to present before us the greatness of our salvation. For if once we see it from God's side and from our side, then we will be able to resist the devil and he will flee from us. We will be able to resist him stead-fastly and fully, and all his suggestions and all he tends to do to us personally in the physical sense. The ultimate way of conquering the devil is really to lay hold of this life that is offered us in the New Testament gospel, and that is the thing to which we are referring here.

According to this statement of our Lord here in his prayer to his Father, one of the objects which he had in view, in doing all the things that we have been looking at in so much detail, was that you and I might have eternal life. The plan in eternity, the laying aside of the glory, the incarnation, the birth in Bethlehem, all he endured for thirty-three years, all his preaching all his miracles, his death upon the cross, his resurrection, the ascension, the sending of the Holy Spirit— one of the great objectives for which all that was designed was that you and I might have eternal life. Here he is at the end, and he prays the Father, 'The hour is come; glorify thy Son, that thy Son also may glorify thee: as thou hast given him power over all flesh, that he should give eternal life to as many as thou hast given him.'

What then is this eternal life of which he speaks? Anyone who reads the New Testament must know at once that it is one of the central themes of the New Testament itself, and especially of this gospel of John. It is the theme above all else which is emphasized by John, not only in this gospel but also in his epistles. Take that well-known verse, John 3:16, 'For

God so loved the world, that he gave his only begotten Son'—why?—'that whosoever believeth in him should not perish'—that is the negative, and here is the positive—'but have everlasting life.' That is it! Again we read of the Lord saying, 'I am come. . .' Why did he come from God? Why did he leave the courts of heaven? Why did he humble himself? Why was he made in the likeness of sinful flesh? The answer is 'that they might have life, and that they might have it more abundantly' (Jn 10:10), And in John 6 you will find that he repeats it frequently: it is the great emphasis.

Paul, too, puts the same point when he says, 'The wages of sin is death; but the gift of God is eternal life through Jesus Christ our Lord' (Rom 6:23). Thus, you see, it is the great central message of the New Testament. Paul is constantly dealing with it: 'Reckon ye also yourselves to be dead indeed unto sin, but alive unto God through Jesus Christ our Lord' (Rom 6:11). This therefore is surely something which we must look at a little more closely, though I can only introduce the subject, because it is, as I have shown you, the great central theme of the New Testament, and obviously no man can even attempt to deal with it fully in just one discourse. I am going to show you certain things which are laid down here concerning the matter, before we go on to attempt to define it in detail.

The first principle that I would lay down is that the essence and the end of salvation is that we should have eternal life. What is a Christian? What is Christianity? The definition of the New Testament is that a Christian is a man who possesses eternal life. Perhaps the best way of emphasizing that is to consider how it is that we hold such a low view of Christianity and the Christian life. What is the average person's conception of a Christian and what makes one a Christian?

There are many strange answers to that question. Some people seem to think of it in terms of country. They still speak about Christian countries and non-Christian countries,

126SAVED IN ETERNITY

as if the whole country could be Christian. Then others think of it in terms of being christened when you were a child, or even baptized when you were an adult. Others think of it in terms of church membership, some action which is taken, some formality, a name on a register showing that you belong to a society or an institution, and they say that makes you a Christian. Others think of it as living a good life, following Christ and his teaching, trying to apply it personally, and getting other people to do the same, imitating his example, emulating the perfect specimen which he has provided for us. I am going up the scale, and that last, I think, is the highest, the best definition of a Christian that man by his own unaided understanding can ever arrive at.

But according to the New Testament, all that does not even begin to make one a Christian, and the world is very often quick to detect the hollowness of the claims in such people who call themselves Christian. I was reading of a distinction which I think was common among many Chinese people in past years. They called all the ordinary foreigners Christians, but others they called 'Jesus people'. What they meant was that they regarded everybody who went to China from the West as Christians, because they came from so-called Christian countries, and most of them claimed that they were Christian. But the Chinese saw that they were often drunkards, and immoral and so on, and they felt that if that was Christianity then they did not want it. But then they found that there were other people who came from the same countries who also called themselves Christians. But these lived a pure, holy kind of life, they seemed to be out to help people, and were altogether different, and the Chinese began to call them 'Jesus people', because they seemed to be like the Lord Jesus Christ himself.

Now that is the way to make the distinction, so I want to go one step further and suggest that to be a Christian (and to know the very essence of Christian salvation), it is not even enough just to believe in the forgiveness of sins. The people I

have been describing may not even have talked about forgiveness of sins, that was not the distinguishing feature.
Because a man talks about forgiveness of sins in the Lord
Jesus Christ, he is not of necessity a Christian, or at any rate
his definition of a Christian is very imcomplete. The essence
and the end of Christian salvation is the possession of eternal
life: 'As thou hast given him power over all flesh'—Why?—
that their sins might be forgiven? No—'that he should give
eternal life to as many as thou hast given him.' That is
what makes the difference, we must never stop short of that.

It is perhaps important that we should hurriedly glance at
the relationship between these two matters. I feel that many
go astray, and that many heresies have crept into the church
at this point, because of the failure to see this. There is indeed
a direct relationship between the forgiveness of sins and eternal life. Perhaps the best way to put it is that we must never
think of the possession of eternal life as something in and of
itself, as something that is directly possible. We must never
think of the possession of eternal life unless we have first of
all considered the forgiveness of sins. I know of many people
today who say they are not interested in the terms justification and sanctification. But you ignore them at your peril,
because the New Testament teaches us that justification and
forgiveness are an absolute essential before you can receive
eternal life. If you try to forget that this love of God first of
all came by the way of forgiveness and justification, you will
find that you are indulging in a false mysticism, and that you
are deluding yourself and doing something that has often led
people into the greatest misery and unhappiness. So while
Christian salvation does not end at forgiveness, it does start
there; there is no short cut to eternal life except via grace,
repentance, justification, and acceptance in the sight of God.
Eternal life is not the same as justification, it is based upon it.
Justification is the preliminary cleansing of the ground.

Let me illustrate this. Take any of the buildings that were
damaged during the war. There they were, crumbling and

ruined, bits of wall standing here and there. Now before a
new building could be put up on that site, the ruins had to be
cleared away, the remaining walls pulled down, the rubbish
taken away, and the site cleared. It is exactly like that in the
Christian life, in this spiritual experience. You cannot possess
eternal life from God, until the ruins caused by sin have been
dealt with, and these can only be dealt with by the death of
the Lord Jesus Christ upon the cross. We need to be reconciled to God before we can receive life from God. We mus
be justified from our sin and guilt in the sight of God befor
he will give us this blessing. It is in this way that we establish
the relationship between the two. If you begin by seeking
this life from God without forgiveness, that is the false way
of mysticism. But on the other hand, you must not stop at
justification, it is the basis on which we are entitled to ask
God for this divine life, which is the essence of Christianity.
John Wesley, for example, found his favourite definition of
Christianity in the title of a book that was written in the
sixteenth century by a Scotsman called Henry Scougal: *The
life of God in the soul of man.* That is it, the possession of the
life of God in one's own soul. That is the essence and the end
of salvation.

But we must proceed to lay down a second proposition,
which is that by nature we all lack this life and are entirely
without it. You notice how our Lord puts it here: 'that he
should give eternal life to as many as thou hast given him'.
The obvious implication there is that apart from this gift we
are all without this life, and here again is something that is
absolutely basic and vital to the whole of the New Testament
position. We can see this, for example, in Ephesians 2:1–3:
'And you hath he quickened, who were dead in trespasses
and sins; wherein in time past ye walked according to the
course of this world, according to the prince of the power of
the air, the spirit that now worketh in the children of dis-
obedience: among whom also we all had our conversation in
times past in the lusts of our flesh, fulfilling the desires of the

flesh and of the mind; and were by nature the children of wrath, even as others.'

That is the condition and the position of the whole of mankind, until we receive this gift from the Lord Jesus Christ.

Now the question that obviously arises at once is this: how did mankind ever come into such a condition? It is important that we should realize that that is the truth about us, for if we do not realize it, then we are utterly dead in trespasses and sins, and the gospel has nothing to say to us, except to convict us of that fact. So the question is, how did man ever get into such a state? And the answer is to be found in Genesis 3—a vitally important and essential chapter. I find there are so many Christian people today who seem to think you can be fully a Christian and shed the first chapters of Genesis. 'There is no need to believe in all that,' they say, 'because scientific knowledge has made it quite impossible.'

But let us see whether that is a tenable position or not. It seems to me that the biblical doctrine all hangs together, and that we will never see the true greatness of Christian salvation until we fully see and realize the nature of man. According to Scripture, the trouble with man by nature is not that he is incomplete but that he is dead. Now evolutionism tells us that man is just evolving out of the animal stage; he obviously has still a great deal of the bestial in him, but he is advancing up to perfection. The trouble is that he has not climbed high enough yet. But if that is true, then I have to cut out a great deal of my Bible, I have to eschew a great deal of that talk about being 'the children of wrath', for the Bible tells me that I am not only incomplete and inadequate, I am positively evil, I am under the wrath of God, I am subject to perdition because of something that is true of me. That is the meaning of the wrath of God. And that is not just Paul's teaching. The Lord Jesus Christ said, 'He that believeth on the Son of God hath everlasting life: and he that believeth not the Son shall not see life; but the wrath of God abideth on him' (Jn 3:36). No one taught this doctrine more clearly than our Lord himself, and that is why he said, 'I am come that they might have life.'

All this, therefore can only be explained truly in terms of what we are told in Genesis. God made man and made him perfect, and then, we are told, God breathed into man the breath of life and he became a living soul. God thus breathed into man something of his own life, and in that state and condition man was a living soul enjoying the life of God and in correspondence with him. But God, you remember, told man that if he wanted to maintain that life he must be obedient. He could eat of all the trees of the garden, except the particular tree of the knowledge of good and evil. But man disobeyed, even though God had warned him what would have to happen. God had said, 'But of the tree of the knowledge of good and evil, thou shalt not eat of it: for in the day that thou eatest thereof, thou shalt surely die' (Gen 2:17); and, remember, death does not only mean physical death, it means, still more, spiritual death, falling out of relationship with God, and out of correspondence with him.

And the account goes on to tell us what happened. Man disobeyed and though hitherto he had delighted in hearing the voice of God in the Garden, the moment he disobeyed, the link was broken and the voice of God frightened him. But God did not stop at that, he threw man out of the Garden and placed cherubim and a flaming sword to prevent man from going back to that perfect life. Left in his own strength and power, man is condemned to a spiritual death. He loses the voice of God, and the possession of life eternal. From there on man is a creature without a knowledge of God. He lives in ignorance, indeed he becomes an enemy of God. He is, the Bible teaches, dead to spiritual things. He does not enjoy or see any point in prayer; doctrine is mere theory to him, not in any way relevant to his life; and, the Bible tells us, he is now of his father the devil, manifesting in his nature and life the characteristics of the devil, the worst of which is enmity against God, and a hatred of him.

Now it seems to me that this doctrine of the fall which I have been putting to you, is an essential part of the biblical doctrine of salvation. Man has lost this eternal life, which is why he is under the curse and wrath of God, and needs to be given this gift of life. This is not something that I have deduced from the Scriptures, you will find it stated explicitly in I Corinthians 15: 'For as in Adam all die, even so in Christ shall all be made alive', and you will find it also in Romans 5. So I suggest to you that the work of the Lord Jesus Christ— the work of which he says here, 'I have finished the work which thou gavest me to do'—cannot be truly understood until we understand this doctrine of the fall. We do not need some human knowledge telling us that we just have to be raised up and so drawn up a little bit higher. No! We need to be delivered from the wrath of God. It is because of the fall that man is dead in trespasses and sins; he is spiritually dead and that is why he is in that condition.

Let me go on to my next proposition, which is that eternal life is a gift from God. That is made very plain by our Lord's words: 'that he should give eternal life to as many as thou hast given him', and I think that this follows very logically from what I have just been saying. There is, indeed a perfect logic and wholeness in scriptural doctrine, and if you trip up over one part, then the whole of the doctrine is going to be involved. Man, though spiritually dead decided to live the life of God, but he could never produce or generate that life for himself. It is impossible, he was not allowed to do so— there was that flaming sword to bar his way back to that life from which he was dismissed. It cannot be done, no man can ever make himself a Christian, for no man can ever produce the Christian life within himself.

Not only that, it is something that we never arrive at, it is something that we never merit. It does not matter what good you may do, you will never win eternal life. You may have spent the whole of your life in doing good works, but I

say that you have no more right to eternal life than the most
dissolute vagrant in the world today. You say you believe in
attending a place of worship and doing good, but I say that if
you are trusting to these things you are condemning yourself. All our righteousness is but as 'filthy rags', our greatest
virtues are ugly and foul in the sight of God, because they are
all tainted by sin. 'The gift of God is eternal life through Jesus
Christ our Lord' (Rom 6:23): we are saved by grace 'through
faith; and that not of yourselves: it is the gift of God' (Eph
2:8). The whole message of the New Testament is the message of the grace of God, the gift to undeserving sinners, and
we only have eternal life when we receive it as a gift.

There is one further point, which is that there is only one
person who can give us the gift and that is the One who is
praying: 'As thou hast given him power over all flesh, that he
should give eternal life to as many as thou hast given him.' It
is Christ alone who can give us this eternal life. Once more
we see the terrible danger of mysticism, or at any rate of the
mysticism which does not make Christ central. There are
many people in the world who are anxious to possess this life
of God. You will find them writing about it, and one of the
most remarkable examples of this has been Aldous Huxley,
who used to be a complete sceptic, but who came to believe
that nothing can save the world but mysticism, and who
became a Buddhist for that reason. Such men believe that
there is this eternal life of God to be had, that what we need
is that life of God in ourselves and that our trouble is that we
have not got it. They are using the same definition as Henry
Scougal, but notice the difference: these people think that
they can get this life of God in themselves without mentioning the Lord Jesus Christ at all. You get it, they say, by
contemplation of the Absolute, by increasingly sinking into
the eternal and being lost in him, because as you do so, you
are receiving life from him.

I do not want to sound unsympathetic. I think it is a good
thing that men and women are beginning to see that man

alone is insufficient. It is all right as far as it goes, but the vital question is, how do you see it? It is possible to talk about sinking into the heart of the Eternal, but it takes many forms and assumes many guises. There are those who tell you that you can know God and begin to share his life immediately just as you are. They say that the moment you begin to feel your need of God all you have to do is to turn to God and he will begin to speak to you. They do not mention the Lord Jesus Christ at all.

But, my friends, it is he and he alone who can give eternal life. He claims it here and Scripture says it everywhere: 'As thou hast given him power over all flesh that he should give eternal life. . .' There is no one else who can give eternal life to man except the Lord Jesus Christ. If it were possible in any other way, why did he ever come to earth? Why did he work as a carpenter? Why did he endure all he endured? Why the death on the cross? Why the agony and the shame and the blood-stained sweat? There is no other way—the whole plan of salvation centres on him. He alone is the giver of eternal life, and we seek life from God in any other way at our greatest and gravest peril. I am not denying that you may have had experiences, but it is my business to proclaim that whatever happiness you may find, whatever release and freedom, whatever guidance, whatever magic, whatever miraculous things may seem to be happening to you, unless you obtain them directly and only through the Son of God, the Lord Jesus Christ, it is not life from God, and you are the victim of a terrible delusion. One day you will awaken to find that that is a fact; it is he and he alone who is the giver and the transmitter of the life of God to the souls of men.

10

The Only True God

John 17:2–3

We have been seeing together that the ultimate purpose of our salvation is that we might have the gift of eternal life; and we have seen that that is the grand object and the final explanation of everything that was planned by the blessed Trinity. So this is obviously the most important thing we can ever consider together, and we began our consideration of it by realizing that it is something which, as we are by nature as the result of sin, we all lack, because we are 'dead in trespasses and sins' (Eph 2:1). And furthermore we saw that it is something which we have to receive as a gift because however wonderful our morality and conduct may be, they will never rise to the level of the eternal life.

The difference between being a Christian and not being a Christian is not one of degree, it is one of essence and quality, so that the most unworthy Christian is in a better position that the best man outside Christianity. Perhaps the best way of understanding all this is to think of it in terms of relationship. It is a question of blood, if you like; the humblest and the most unworthy member of the royal family is in a more advantageous position from the standpoint of social arrangements in most countries than the greatest and most able person outside that family. A man outside the royal family may be much more cultured, may be a finer

135

specimen of humanity in every respect, yet on all state occasions and great occasions, he has to follow after the humblest and the least worthy member of the royal family. How do you assess his position? You do not assess it in terms of ability and achievement, you assess it in terms of blood relationship. Now that is precisely what the New Testament says about the Christian. He is one who had become a partaker of the divine nature; he is in an entirely new relationship; he has a new nature and quality; a new order of life has entered into him.

Furthermore, we found that it is our Lord alone who can give it to us, and that is what he is emphasizing here. He asks God to glorify him because, he says, in effect, 'If you do not glorify me by enabling me to do this last bit of work which I have to do, if you do not enable me to be a Sin-Bearer of the whole guilt and sin of the world, then the whole of mankind will remain dead in trespasses and sins.' He pleads with and urges his Father to glorify him so that he can give eternal life. So any attempt, as we have seen, to arrive at God, and have communion and fellowship with him, except in and through Christ and all his work, is a snare and delusion.

We now come on to deal with some practical questions. We saw that by definition a Christian is one who has eternal life, so what is this life, and how can one obtain it? I want to take that second question first because it seems to me to be the one that is dealt with first of all in these verses that we are considering. Verse 3 says, 'And this is life eternal, that they might know thee the only true God, and Jesus Christ, whom thou hast sent.' What does that mean exactly? Is it a definition of what is meant by eternal life, or is it a description of the way in which eternal life is to be obtained? Those are the two possible explanations and expositions.

I suppose that in an ultimate sense it is right to say that both are true, and yet I find myself, on the whole, agreeing with those who think that it is probably a description of the way in which etrnal life is to be obtained. Now John has his own style of writing and you will find he always puts things in this particular way. Let me give you an illustration of this same thing from John 3:19 where he says, 'And this is the condemnation, that light is come into the world, and men loved darkness rather than light. . .' Notice what an exact parallel that is with this statement: 'And this is life eternal, that they might know thee the only true God, and Jesus Christ, whom thou hast sent.' It is the same form of expression so that John 3:19 is probably a safe guide to follow in the interpretation of this verse.

Let me explain. When John says, 'this is the condemnation', he is not giving us a definition of the condemnation; rather he is telling us the cause of it, which is 'that light is come into the world, and men loved darkness rather than light'. Surely, therefore, this verse can be interpreted in the same way. This is the thing that causes, or leads to life eternal —'that they might know thee the only true God, and Jesus Christ, whom thou hast sent'. I can give you further examples and illustrations of the same thing. John says in his first epistle, 'This is the true God and eternal life' (1 Jn 5:20) by which he means, 'This is the true God, and the cause of eternal life'—referring again to the Lord Jesus Christ. So we have here primarily an account of the way, or the means, by which eternal life is to be obtained. Or, if you prefer it, we have here a description of the origin of eternal life rather than a definition of its essence. Yet, as I have said, it is very difficult to separate these two things from each other: that which gives me eternal life is the eternal life itself, for as I receive and enjoy the means of obtaining eternal life, I am obtaining it at the same time. However, we should hold these things as separate ideas in our mind.

Let us look therefore at the mechanism by which eternal life comes to us. As we do so, God grant that we all may realize that this is not only our greatest need, but also the most wonderful privilege that can ever come to us men and women. By giving us his eternal life God is saying that we can have the right and the authority to become sons of God, that we may indeed and in truth become partakers of the divine nature, and that we may have, here, at this moment, a true reminder in our earthly course of this relationship to God that is going to make us heirs of God and joint heirs with Christ. God has given us his nature, and not even death and the grave can rob us of our heritage. It not only means a transformed life while we are still here in this world, it is a guarantee of such great things.

How, then, are we to get eternal life? Well, the essential thing we are told here is that it is ultimately a question of knowing God, and that is of course the great question that is held before us everywhere in the Bible. God is Someone who is to be known by us, and there is no possibility of eternal life apart from this knowledge of him. John says this in his first epistle. He has become an old man and is at the point of death, and he tells the people to whom he is writing that he wants them to be happy, and to be sharing the same joy that fills his heart. There is a joy possible in this life, he says. Your joy can be full in this world, and it is a joy that is based upon fellowship with God. We have a wonderful fellowship to share, and truly 'our fellowship is with the Father, and with his Son Jesus Christ' (1 Jn 1:3). You notice how these New Testament writers repeat themselves, and they do this because they are always talking about this wonderful fact; a man who knows anything about this intimate fellowship with God cannot stop speaking about it. We can all speak about the things that interest us, we go on talking about them, and here is the greatest thing of all, eternal life, knowing God and having fellowship with him—it is no wonder that they keep repeating themselves!

How then do we know God? The Lord Jesus Christ divides it up into two main headings, and I merely want to consider them briefly now. He says, 'This is eternal life, that they might know thee the only true God', and he puts it like this because he is issuing a warning, or, if you like, he is stating this truth in the form of a contrast. He is emphasizing that we must be absolutely certain that the God in whom we believe, the God whom we claim to know, is the only true God. Now by using these words 'only' and 'true' he is clearly presenting God to our consideration as over and against something else, and it is obvious that he is warning against idols and false gods.

You find a great deal about that in the New Testament. John, again, ends his first epistle with these words, 'Little children, keep yourselves from idols.' That is the last word of this old man as he writes his farewell letter to the infant churches. He starts by saying that nothing matters but that we have fellowship with God the Father and with his Son Jesus Christ; he then goes on to warn them against certain heresies, and he sums it all up by saying, 'Keep yourselves from idols.' And the warning is as necessary today as it was in the first century. We must be absolutely certain that the God we worship is the only true and living God. Paul, also, in writing to the Thessalonians reminds them of how, when he first preached the gospel to them, they 'turned from idols to serve the living and true God' (1 Thess 1:9)—that is it. Again, the account in Acts 17 of Paul's visit to Athens tells us how that cultured city was full of temples to the various gods. The people of Athens were too 'religious' in a sense, worshipping all these gods, Mercury, Jupiter, Mars and then, lest any should be left out, there was a curious temple 'To the unknown God'. And yet the whole time they were ignorant of God himself. 'Whom, therefore,' says Paul, 'ye ignorantly worship, him declare I unto you' (Acts 17:23). That is the great business of the Bible, to hold before us the only true and living God.

And, let me repeat, this is as essential today as it was in the first century. It is not, perhaps, that we worship those old pagan deities, but we have a tendency today to worship philosophic abstractions in the same way as they did. You find people today writing in very learned terms about the

Absolute or the Ultimate, or the Source of all being, or the life in the universe. God, to so many people, is nothing but a sheer abstraction, nothing but a philosophical concept, and when they speak of God it is of some kind of philosophical 'X': God is to so many some great force or energy. The Bible is constantly warning us against all that, and, as in the words of our Lord here to his Father, the Bible is always calling us to realize that there is only one true God.

Then there are certain things we must know about him before we can possibly have fellowship with him, and before we can receive life from him. First, obviously, we must believe he is a person. That is a very difficult concept, and yet it is vital and essential. God says, 'I AM that I AM'; God is God, and God, therefore, is a person. The author of Hebrews puts it like this in a very important passage in his epistle. He is talking about the life of faith, and about the secret of men like Moses and others who went through the world as great heroes, mastering their circumstances, and standing out above all the average men in this life—what, he asks, was their secret? And the answer he gives is that their secret was faith, and their relationship to God. Yes, but if you want to be in that full relationship to God, there is one absolute condition—'He that cometh to God must believe that he is, and that he is a rewarder of them that diligently seek him' (Heb 11:6).

You see, when you come to God, you must not come in the wrong way. There was a poem which was very popular and often quoted some years ago, which ran:

> Out of the night that covers me,
> Black as the pit from pole to pole,
> I thank whatever gods there be
> For my unconquerable soul.
>
> *W. E. Henley*

Rubbish! That is the very kind of nonsense against which the Bible warns us. If you come to God and really want to know and please him, you do not come in this mood of 'whatever gods there be'. No, 'He that cometh to God must believe that he is, and that he is a rewarder of them that diligently seek him.' That is inevitably our starting point. God is a living God, not a concept or abstraction or term in a philosophical category. If you want a perfect exposition of that, you should read the accounts which are given in the Old Testament of some of the false gods that people worshipped. I commend to your study Isaiah 46, where the prophet mocks at the false god Baal that the foolish children of Israel had been worshipping. They had to carry him from one place to another because he could not walk! Why worship such a god when you have a God who will carry you? asks Isaiah. Or what about the description of false gods in Psalm 115? 'Eyes have they, but they see not: they have ears, but they hear not: noses have they, but they smell not . . . they that make them are like unto them' (verses 6–8).

There you have one of the most glorious bits of sarcasm in the whole of Scripture.

And the verse which we are considering here is urging us to start by a preliminary realization of this same tremendous truth—that he is the living God, he is the Creator. In all our preoccupation with God the Saviour, we must never forget God the Creator. God is our Saviour but he is also the Lord of the universe. He is the One who said, 'Let there be light: and there was light.' He has brought everything into being. He is in the heavens and everything is at his feet. So we must remember that we start with the Lord of the universe, the Creator, the Instigator of everything that is.

And then we must come on to a consideration of his character. 'God is light,' says John in his first epistle, 'and in him is no darkness at all' (1 Jn 1:5). Before you drop on your knees next time and begin to speak to God, before you seek him and his face and this life he has come to give, never fail to remind yourself of these things. Try to remember his greatness and his majesty and his might, and then go on to remember that he is life, that he is holy, that he is righteous, that he is just, and that he is of such a pure countenance that he cannot even look upon evil. Remember that you are speaking to the Judge of the whole world. All these things are emphasized by this little phrase 'the only true God'. He is not like those false gods, those abstractions. You are going into the presence of the eternal God, a living God, One who is, who always has been, the Great I AM from eternity to eternity. That is the essential starting point and, I repeat, until we have that clear in our minds and in our understanding our prayer to God is probably nothing but a mere crying out to him in desperation. God, if I may so put it, has taken the trouble to reveal himself to us—that is the whole point of the Old Testament—so we have no right to go to God in ignorance, we must make use of the knowledge he has given us. He says that he is a jealous God, emphasizing his personal quality, and that he will not allow us to have any other gods beside him: 'Thou shalt worship the Lord thy God, and him only shalt thou serve' (Lk 4:8). We must, therefore, take the trouble to get hold of this knowledge and information. We must really wrestle with this revelation and then, in the light of that, come to God believing that he is. It is not that we understand his absolute qualities, but we realize that we are speaking to One who has called himself, Father, and who wants us to come to him in that way.

But we do not stop at that. 'He that cometh to God must believe that he is', yes, but he must also believe that 'he is a rewarder of them that deligently seek him' (Heb 11:6)—which is put here in John 17 in this way: 'And this is life eternal, that they might know thee the only true God, and Jesus Christ, whom thou hast sent.' This is obviously crucial, and in its essence it means that we must not only know him as the only true God, we must also know him as the God of our salvation, because unless we know him in this second sense, we will never obtain eternal life from him. I can put it like this. We have seen that our Lord's first warning is against the false gods, a warning to the Gentiles, and this second warning is a warning to the Jews, to people who only think of God in terms of the Old Testament, and who still go to God as if the New Testament had never been given to us. They come to God only in terms of law and have never come into the relationship of grace, and because of that, they are going to rob themselves of the greatest and the chief blessing of salvation.

That is the glory of our Bible, we have the Old and New Testaments, and may I emphasize again the vital importance of taking *both*. It is quite wrong to take the Old Testament alone, and there is a sense in which it is almost equally wrong to take the New Testament alone. It was the Holy Spirit that guided the early church to interpret the two together. We must remember that God is the Creator, and also the Saviour; and, too, we must remember that he is not only the Saviour he is the sole Creator—we worship a blessed triune God.

But here the emphasis is upon God as life, God not only as he is in and of himself, but in his relationship to the world and especially in his relationship to man. We must realize as we approach God that his ultimate, gracious purpose with regard to man has been revealed to us, and it is a purpose of love and mercy, and of kindness and compassion. And, as we have seen, this is something that is only known fully and finally in and through the Lord Jesus Christ. That is why this statement must be put like this, 'This is life eternal that they may know thee the only true God, and Jesus Christ, whom thou hast sent.' This truth is an absolute necessity. That is why our Lord said, 'I am the way, the truth, and the life: no man cometh unto the Father but by me' (Jn 14:6). He is the way to God, he is the truth about God, and apart from the life he gives us, we will never share or know the life of God. So there is no knowledge of God apart from him, through him comes this ultimate true and saving knowledge, the saving relationship.

Of course, every word in this statement has supreme significance. You notice what this verse tells us about the Lord Jesus Christ—'That they might know thee the only true God, *and* Jesus Christ. . .' At once we are told there that he is equal with God, for immediately this man, Christ Jesus, is put into the same category as the only true and living God. Here is One who is on the face of this earth but who can be bracketed with God the Father. Some foolish people, such as the Unitarians, have often tried to use this phrase in order to prove their particular theory. They say that there is only one God and that Jesus Christ was not God, and they try to prove is by saying that Christ himself, while he was in the world, said that there is only one true God. But they stop at that point and forget this vital thing, that the One who says those words, 'the only true God, and Jesus Christ. . .', immediately puts himself into the same position as God. Here is One who is co-equal with God and co-eternal with God. Here is One who is God himself, God the Son, ever eternally in the bosom of the Father—'and Jesus Christ. . .' Thus we are fully entitled to make this statement that God is not only eternal and true but cannot be fully and finally known except in and through One who thus adds himself, as it were, to him.

Then here is the name, *Jesus*, which reminds us of the truth of the incarnation that this eternal Son of God was made man—the man Jesus. But the man Jesus is One who is God and who is co-equal with him and whom, therefore, you think of in terms of God and with God—'and Jesus'.

But he is also Jesus *Christ*, and 'the Christ' means the Messiah, the One who has been anointed to do this special work of bringing men to God and of giving God's life to man. You see how all this mighty doctrine is put here as it were in a nutshell for us—'and Jesus Christ'. It is all there—the ultimate object is to know this only true God; yes, and the way to know him is to know Jesus Christ.

Our Lord goes on to say, 'O righteous Father, the world

hath not known thee: but I have known thee, these [disciples] have known that thou hast sent me' (verse 25). And because they know that thou hast sent me, they know the Father and they have eternal life.

So we must realize that Jesus Christ gives us the revelation of God as no one else can give it. 'No man hath seen God at any time; the only begotten Son, which is in the bosom of the Father, he hath declared him' (Jn 1:18). He has manifested and revealed him, he has taught us about him. Yes, but you see he has gone further, as we have already seen. He has not only declared him, he has also taken out of the way the things that prevented our being in communion with him, he has removed the barrier of sin. If he had not done that, the knowledge and the revelation would avail us nothing.

But I just want to take one final step before we end this study. So far we have found that the knowledge of God is based upon these statements. It is based first upon the Old Testament revelation of God, the God who has differentiated himself from all the pagan gods and idols, the only true God who has revealed himself in the Ten Commandments and the moral law and the prophets. We then go on to the revelation of the Lord Jesus Christ and all that he has revealed, which makes him say, 'He that hath seen me hath seen the Father' (Jn 14:9). We have seen that he also removes the barrier of sin, the thing that comes between us and God and blinds our eyes and minds to the vision of God.

But he even goes a step beyond that. The Lord Jesus Christ gives us eternal life in a still deeper way. He gives us eternal life not only by giving us a knowledge about God, but by giving us the very life of God himself. This, says John, is the true God, the eternal life. We have seen, too, how Paul puts it: 'As in Adam all die, even so in Christ shall all be made alive' (1 Cor 15:22). Of course, this is a profound doctrine. We have all fallen because we are all 'in Adam'. Adam was the first man, the father of the human race, and the entire human race and the whole of humanity was in him. The result was that when Adam fell the whole race of man fell. He was not only the representative, we were in him, in his line, and death has come upon us all because we are in Adam, and because of what we have inherited from him.

Now over and against that, the New Testament puts the Lord Jesus Christ, and its amazing doctrine is that every true Christian is related to Christ, as every natural man was related to Adam. In other words, it means that if we are Christian, if we believe in the Lord Jesus Christ, we are incorporated into him, we become part of him, we share his life, and we are born of him. We are in him in exactly the same way as we were in Adam. This is the special work of the Holy Spirit. It is he who quickens us and brings about our regeneration. It is he who unites us to Christ and makes us a part of the life of Christ, and it is in that way, by sharing the life of Christ himself, that we receive the gift of eternal life. That is why he is so absolutely vital and essential. It is not something outside him, he gives us eternal life by giving us himself, and by this mystic union with Christ, by this relationship to him, we become participators of his own life. We are partakers of the divine nature, we have fellowship with God and the life of God enters into our souls.

So this is eternal life, this is the means of eternal life, 'that they might know thee the only true God, and Jesus Christ, whom thou hast sent.'

If we know this Christ, if we believe on him, we have eternal life, we have already become the sons of God.

11

A New Principle

John 17:2–3

In the light of our two preceding studies, the question which each one of us should be asking before we go any furher is this: do I possess eternal life? Have I received the gift of eternal life? It is the most momentous question we can ever ask ourselves in this life, because our eternal destiny depends upon our answer to it. That is the message of the Bible everywhere, from beginning to end. It emphasizes a Day of Judgement when certain great books will be opened, and unless our names are written in the Lamb's book of life— which means that we are possessors of eternal life—we go to destruction, to damnation and to eternal punishment. Clearly, therefore, this is the most important matter of all, and not only from the standpoint of our eternal destiny. Of course, we have to put that first, because it is the most serious matter, but it is also important from the standpoint of our life in this world, and the enjoyment and the success of that life, in the highest sense.

So, then, we have found that this life becomes possible to us only in and through a knowledge of God in the Lord Jesus Christ, and we have seen, too, that he enables us to know God by imparting himself to us, through the Holy Spirit. By entering into us and giving us life, he enables us to know God, and that is the point at which we start, when we discover the way to this life, the way in which it is obtained.

It is necessary, perhaps, that I should emphasize this word 'know'—'that they might *know* thee'—in order to bring out clearly that that does not mean merely an intellectual awareness. This word 'know' is a strong and powerful word. It does not just mean that you are acquainted with or aware of something; it does not even mean an intellectual acceptance of a number of propositions; it is much deeper than that. When God spoke to the Children of Israel through the prophet Amos, he said, 'You only have I known of all the families of the earth' (Amos 3:2). Obviously that does not mean that God was not aware of the existence of other nations; this word 'know' is a word which means 'you only have I known in an intimate way', you are the only people, in a sense, in whom I have been particularly interested. That is how this word is constantly used in Scripture and that is its meaning here. The knowledge of God about which our Lord speaks here means an actual living realization of him, not just believing in the being and existence of God, but knowing him as One who is living and dwelling in us. It is a living knowledge, and we must be careful that we do not attach a meaning to this word which falls short of that exalted conception.

Having said that, we now go forward to consider exactly what that means. We have seen the way in which we obtain eternal life. If a man really does not know God in Christ in that intimate sense, he has not got it. But what is this life which is claimed in that way? The first thing which we must emphasize is that it is a quality of life. Eternal life must be conceived of in terms of quality rather than mere quantity, or duration. That does not mean that the element of length and duration does not enter in, because it does. But over and above that, is this question of the quality—the thing that is always emphasized in the Scriptures. Our Lord puts it like this: 'I am come that they might have life, and that they might have it *more abundantly*' (Jn 10:10). So we see that, according to Scripture, what is offered to us is a type and kind of life which is available to us at this present time and which will go on right through the remainder of our lives in this world, and, still more important, beyond death and the grave and into eternity. That is really what is meant by eternal life.

Now both these aspects need to be emphasized. The astounding thing, in other words, is that the Christian is one who can receive here in this world, now in the present, something of the very life of glory itself. The apostle Paul speaks of that in Romans 8:23, where he refers to himself as one of those who have received the 'firstfruits', or, as he says, who have received a kind of foretaste. You see what is in his mind?

It is like the first gleanings of the crop. You go out into your garden and you pick the first raspberries, the full crop will soon come, but here is a preliminary instalment. You have the first fruits, the foretaste; you do not have it all, but you have a handful of what you are going to receive in an ultimate, complete fullness. And that is the way in which the Christian comes into eternal life, and it is surely one of the most remarkable and astounding things we can ever realize, that here on earth we can begin to experience something of the life of heaven, something of the life of glory.

Now the time element comes in like this. Though we receive the life itself here in this world, because we are in the flesh, and because of the imperfection that sin has introduced into every part of our being, there is a kind of limit. The apostle Paul makes this plain in writing to the Corinthians, 'For now,' he says, 'we see through a glass, darkly. . .' (1 Cor 13:12). Some people say it should be translated, 'we see in a sort of riddle', but that does not matter, both show that we do see after a fashion. But then note the difference: 'For now we see through a glass, darkly; but *then face to face.*' There is a certain amount of distortion in what we see at the present time we are seeing the real thing but 'darkly'. Then we shall see it even as it is, '. . .then shall I know even as also I am known.' 'Now,' Paul says again, 'I know in part'; it is the difference, says the apostle, between the knowledge of a child and the knowledge of a grown up person. The child has, in a sense, a real knowledge, but it is an elementary and an imperfect one. 'When I was a child, I spake as a child, I understood as a child, I thought as a child: but when I became a man, I put away childish things' (1 Cor 12:11). That is exactly the difference, says Paul, between eternal life in this world and eternal life as we shall enjoy it in the glory. The life is the same, only here it is partial, and imperfect 'as in a glass darkly'. But thank God that this is what is offered to us even in this life and world. We can begin the life of glory here on earth: 'Celestial fruits on earthly ground may grow,' says the hymn writer, and that is the thing that our Lord would have us realize constantly as Christian people.

Very well, let us hold these two elements in our minds. It is a quality of life, and that quality is the life of heaven, the life of glory itself. We start it here, we can have it now and it will continue, it will grow, it will increase, and ultimately it will blossom out into that life of perfection when we shall see with an utterly open face and 'know even as also we are known' by him. I think that this is one of the most thrilling things a man can ever learn in this life, so I summarize it by putting it like this: It is possible for us as Christian people, to receive here and now something of that life which the Lord Jesus Christ himself enjoyed. He enjoyed this eternal life while he was here on earth, and what he offers and what he gives, he tells us, is something of that life—'that he should give eternal life to as many as thou hast given him'.

So, then, having described it in general, let us try to understand it a little more personally and see what exactly is true of this life. Let me give you some of the New Testament definitions of it. We are told that as a result of having this life we become sons of God, or children of God—'For ye are all the children of God,' says the apostle Paul in Galatians 3:26. Another phrase, used by John in his first epistle, is that we are 'born of God' (1 Jn 5:1) and in John 3:8 we read that we are 'born of the Spirit'. The apostle Peter describes it by saying that we become 'partakers of the divine nature' (2 Pet 1:4)—an astounding statement. In another place he tells us that we are 'begotten again' (1 Pet 1:3), we are regenerated. Now all those terms, and others too, are used in the New Testament in order to give us some conception and under-standing of the quality and nature of eternal life. And it was in order to give us this marvellous life that the Lord Jesus Christ came into the world. That is why he went to the cross, that is why he was buried and rose again, it was that you and I might become sons of God, children of God, born of God, partakers of the divine nature, that we might be regenerated, and made anew, and receive a new life. But, I must hasten to add, it is very important that we should not misconstrue any of these great, exalted terms.

Not one of them means that you and I become divine. We do not cease to be human. We are not turned into gods. We must never put such a meaning to those great terms. It does not mean that the divine essence, as it were, is infused into us. I put it in this negative form because some of the mystics have crossed the line and have taught—indeed you will find it very often in Roman Catholic teaching—that the divine nature is infused into us. That is something which is in the background of their doctrine of transubstantiation. Now there is no such teaching in the Bible and it savours of the monastic, and of Greek philosophy; we must be careful not to interpret those terms as meaning that we actually become divine. We are still human, though we are partakers of the divine nature.

I would even go beyond that. When you and I are in heaven and in glory, when our very bodies shall have been glorified and every vestige of sin shall have been purged out of us, when we shall see him face to face and be like him,

even then we shall still be men. The Lord Jesus is God-Man.
We never become God-men. We still remain man, but glorified man, perfect man. We are not transfigured or transformed into God.

This is obviously a very high and difficult doctrine to
understand, and I suppose that we are not meant to understand it fully in this life and world. The safe way of express-
ing it is to say that what happens to us when we receive
eternal life is that something entirely new comes into us and
into our life and experience. The Scripture says we become
new men, a new creation. The New Testament refers to a
new man and an old man, and we are told to put off the old
and to put on the new man. A new principle of life comes
into us which produces a profound change in us, and gives
us, therefore, a new quality of life and being. This new
principle produces in us a new nature, a new outlook, so
much so that having received it, we are able to say with
Paul—and he knows exactly what he means when he says
it—'If any man be in Christ, he is a new creature'—a new
creation —'old things are passed away; behold, all things are
become new' (2 Cor 5:17). It is all because of this principle
that enters into our lives.

I am tempted to say a word at this point about the
relationship of this new principle to the natural qualities and
faculties of man, because people are often in trouble and
difficulty about that. They wonder what happens when a
man receives this new life, what happens when he is born
again. Is he given an entirely new faculty or a new set of
faculties? The answer, of course, is, no. What he receives is a
new principle that affects all his faculties. Let me explain
what I mean. This new principle is something apart from
our faculties but it affects all of them. It is, as it were, something that comes in and enlivens them and enables us to use
them in an entirely different manner. Now that is very important for this reason: the Christian life, the receiving of this
eternal life, is absolutely independent of our natural faculties,

and qualities—and let us thank God for that fact. We all differ, for example, we all differ intellectually some are born with a greater ability to understand, with better brains, than others; some are able to read and understand what they read better than others. There is an endless variety and variation in people by nature, from the standpoint of propensities and abilities. The glory of this eternal life is that it can come into the life of any kind of person, and it really does not depend in any sense upon their individual qualities and faculties. The result is that a person who is unintelligent can receive this principle of new life quite as much as the most intelligent person in the world. And, furthermore, he can be as spiritual as that intelligent person. It is a principle apart from the natural faculties.

But of course it is at the same time a principle that can use the natural faculties. That is why when God wants a great teacher of the Christian gospel, he chooses a man like the apostle Paul. Yes, but Paul was no more a Christian than the most ignorant person in the church at Corinth. It is the *principle* that matters—we must not merely consider this in terms of understanding and ability, it is something much more wonderful and glorious than that. And that is why Paul was able to say in 1 Corinthians 1:21: 'For after that in the wisdom of God the world by wisdom knew not God, it pleased God by the foolishness of preaching to save them that believe.' God, he says, takes the ignorant and by means of them he confounds the wise, and he takes the weak and confounds the mighty—because of this new principle which he introduces. What, then, is the effect of the introduction of this principle? This life eternal, about which we are speaking, is, as I have said, something which affects the entire man. But it is especially interesting to observe the way in which it affects a man's understanding and apprehension of spiritual things. And the way to look at that is to contrast the natural, unregenerate man, who is not a Christian, with the man who is a Christian. According to Scripture, the natural man is spiritually dead. May I be so bold as to put it like this: if there is anybody to whom these things about which I am speaking are really utterly meaningless, then, as I understand Scripture, it means that such a person is spiritually dead and has not received eternal life, because, as Paul puts it, 'The natural man receiveth not the things of the Spirit of God: for they are foolishness unto him' (1 Cor 2:14). They are meaningless to him, they are like a foreign language, and he is bored by them.

Paul works this out in great detail in 1 Corinthians 2. He says that we, as Christians, have not received 'the spirit of the world, but the spirit which is of God', and we will never know them until we receive the Spirit. 'Eye hath not seen,' he says, 'nor ear heard, neither have entered into the heart of man, the things which God hath prepared for them that love him' (verse 9). And these things about which Paul is speaking do not refer to heaven, but to things here on earth. However, Paul goes on, we understand because 'the Spirit searcheth all things, yea, the deep things of God' (verse 10). Now that, I think, is something wonderful and glorious. The princes of this world do not understand these things, and let us remember that when he is talking of princes, he is not only referring to people who are crowned kings, he is including the philosophers, he is talking about the Greeks who sought and worshipped wisdom. When Paul says that the princes of this world do not know the Lord Jesus Christ, he means they do not understand or grasp the truth because they are spiritually dead. Living in terms of their natural powers and faculties, they come to these spiritual things with their natural intellect and they see nothing in them. And he goes on to say that they never will see anything in them until they have received the light of the Spirit. But, he says, 'he that is spiritual judgeth'—which means he understands, he can evaluate all things—'yet he himself is judged of no man' (verse 15). The Christian is an enigma to the non-Christian, the Christian does not really understand himself! He has an understanding and an insight which the other man does not have.

Then there is the wonderful statement at the end of the chapter, 'For who hath known the mind of the Lord, that he may instruct him?' And Paul gives this amazing answer— 'But we have the mind of Christ.' He does not mean by this that we have the perfect knowledge that Christ has. He means that we have the spiritual understanding of Christ himself. He has given it to us, and we have received it as a gift from him. It is one of the aspects of eternal life—the mind of Christ. And this means that the new man, the man who has received this gift of eternal life, has an interest in spiritual things. The other man has not got this, but the new man has, and he begins to look at himself in a new way. He realizes that he is not merely an animal sent into this world to eat and drink and sleep and make money. No! He realizes that he is a spiritual being. He knows within himself that there is something which lifts him up beyond the whole universe, that he is meant for God and that he has God's Spirit within him. He did not know that before, but he knows it now. He has an entirely new view of death as well as of life and he faces his life in this world in an entirely new way.

My dear friends, if you want to know whether you have eternal life, that is a simple way of deciding it. When you think about yourself do you stop merely at the point at which the man of the world stops, or do you remind your-self every day of your life that you have a soul, a spirit; that what really matters is not this brief span of life in this world, but that destiny for which we are meant, that life that is awaiting us with God, that glory to which we are going? The Christian views himself with a spiritual mind and he faces God in an entirely different way.

The Christian also has an entirely different view of the world in which he lives, it is a spiritual view. What is your view of the world at this moment? Are you troubled or

grieved about it? Are you hurt by it? Paul says of the
Christian that 'we that are in this tabernacle do groan, being
burdened' (2 Cor 5:4). Or again, even we 'which have
received the firstfruits of the Spirit, even we ourselves groan
within ourselves, waiting for the adoption, to wit, the
redemption of our body' (Rom 8:23). Does the world
trouble you? You see, if you have received eternal life you
become like the Lord Jesus Christ. In this world he was a
man of sorrows and acquainted with grief because he saw
what sin had done to his Father's great and glorious world,
because he saw men and women in the shackles of sin and
dupes in the service of Satan. It grieved him at heart and the
man who is spiritually minded knows something of that
view of this life and world, and of the men and women who
are in it.

In other words, spiritual things become real to the man
who receives eternal life. These things are not theoretical to
him, they are not merely philosophical or academic. He does
not feel that they are something he has to force himself to
take up. They are the centre of his life, the most vital things
of all to him. Do we have to force ourselves to think about
these things? Do we have to say, 'It is Sunday again and I
suppose I had better do so and so?' Or do we delight in it,
wishing, in a way, that we could spend every day looking
into these things? Do we hunger and thirst after righteousness? Are these to us the most vital, momentous, central
things? They are to the spiritual man, and they must be,
because of what has happened to him. The principle of the
life of Christ has come into him and he becomes like Christ.

And the last thing I would say about him is that he has an
understanding of spiritual things which he never had before.
John, in his first epistle, warns those first Christians against
certain dangers and heresies. There is, he says, a sense in
which he need not keep on reminding them, because they
'have an unction from the Holy One' (1 Jn 2:20). It is true of
the Christian: he has a spiritual understanding of spiritual

things, he knows the truth about the Lord Jesus Christ. There are people who are always arguing about the person of Christ. They are always in trouble and want to understand this, that and the other. But the spiritual man is not like that. I do not mean that he can necessarily explain everything to you. Look at those Corinthian Christians, the people of whom Paul said that they had 'the mind of Christ'. They were not great philosophers, for, he says, 'not many mighty . . . are called'. And yet you know they could see the Lord Jesus Christ in a way that the princes of this world could not. The Christian is the man who does not understand intellectually, he understands spiritually; he knows because of this principle of life that is come into him—life recognizes life.

The knowledge which is given to the Christian is almost an instinctive knowledge. I think the best analogy is this. It is comparable to the knowledge which a man has who is in love with a woman. It is not possible for him to sit down and write out a philosophical account of his love, he cannot explain it rationally: he knows it, but here his reason ceases. The great love which reason and knowledge do not understand—that is it. We know, because we have love and love recognizes love, and love attracts love. The little lamb cannot give you a rational reason why it should pick out one sheep as its mother but it knows that sheep is his mother. The Christian's knowledge of his Lord is something like that, he *knows* and he knows the way of salvation. People say, 'I cannot understand why one man had to die on the cross for all,' but the Christian does understand. He cannot fully understand the doctrine of the atonement, but he is not in any trouble over the fact that the sins of the world were laid upon the innocent body of the Son of God. He has the mind of Christ and an understanding of these things by means of this unction of the Holy Spirit. Spiritual truths are not strange to him, they are life, they are everything. He delights in them, he lives by them and his one desire is to know more and more. Have you received 'eternal life'? It is a gift, he gives it, he has done everything so that you may have it. You find that the things that used to interest you now carry no meaning to you, and these other things become the only things that matter.

> Perish every fond ambition,
> All I've sought, and hoped, and known;
> Yet how rich is my condition—
> God and heaven are still my own!
>
> *Henry Francis Lyte*

The moment a man receives this life he becomes a kind of stranger in this world. They are pilgrims, strangers, sojourners, men who have their eyes set and fixed upon 'the glory that remains', though living still in this world of sin and shame.

God grant that we all may know that we have eternal life. If you know that you have not, confess it to God and ask him to give it to you by his Spirit. If you have it, dwell upon it that you may grow in grace and in the knowledge of God, and be changed from glory into glory even as you look at it and contemplate it.

12

Filled with Life Anew

John 17:2–3

As we have been considering the eternal life which we receive through our Lord Jesus Christ, we have seen that it is
something that we cannot analyse too carefully or too
closely. The danger is always that we stop short at certain
points such as forgiveness and assurance without realizing
that we are really called to share this life of God.
Christianity, we reminded ourselves, in the terms of the
definition of the Scotsman, Henry Scougal, is 'The life of
God in the soul of man'. So the object of all our endeavours,
of all our worship, of our prayers and of our Bible reading,
indeed, of everything we do, should be to experience what is
expressed in that old hymn.

> Breathe on me, Breath of God,
> Fill me with life anew,
> That I may love what Thou dost love,
> And do what Thou wouldst do.
>
> *Edwin Hatch*

and nothing less than that. And here we are reminded of this
glorious objective towards which we should all be striving
and which should be the supreme desire of our lives.

We have been looking at only one aspect of the radical
manner in which eternal life manifests itself in our life and

living, namely, the ways in which it affects our thought, our outlook and our attitude—the difference, if you like, that it makes to us in an intellectual sense. We must now go on to consider certain other manifestations of this glorious and wondrous life which God gives to us through our Lord and Saviour Jesus Christ. He is sent from heaven to earth, to the cross and the grave, to the resurrection and the ascension, in order that he might give eternal life to those whom God has already given him. There is a sense in which the best way of looking at it is to say that those who have this eternal life begin to live the kind of life that the Lord Jesus Christ himself lived; that is perhaps the most accurate definition of it. We are meant to be living the kind of life that he lived, for, let us never forget, while he never ceased to be God, he became truly man as well. He is God and man, He is perfect man as well as perfect God, and what he says here is that he has come in order to give the type of life which he lived to those whom God has given him. So, then, as we come to examine the kind of life which we live, we who possess this eternal life, the best way of doing so is to look at the life of our Lord himself, and to see that the principles which characterized his life should be the very principles that animate and characterize our own.

Again, I have selected certain principles. The obvious one —and we touched on this in our last study—is that the man who has received the gift of eternal life knows God. It is not only that he knows things about God, it is not even that he believes certain things concerning God, it is beyond that, he *knows* God. You cannot read the gospels and their accounts of the life of our Lord without seeing that this was clearly the fundamental and the basic thing in his life here on earth as man. He knew God. He keeps on saying it—'I thank thee, O Father, Lord of heaven and earth, because thou hast hid these things from the wise and prudent, and hast revealed them unto babes. Even so, Father: for so it seemed good in thy sight' (Mt 11:25,26). He says, 'Neither knoweth any man the

Father, save the Son. . .' (Mt 11:27). God was not some
stranger in the far distance; no, he knew him with an intimacy and frankness which enabled him always to come into
his presence. He seemed to be longing to be there at all
times. And all that is something which is offered to the
Christian. He is meant to know God, by which I mean that
God becomes real to him. God is not merely an intellectual
concept to the man who has eternal life, he becomes an
actuality and a reality. He really does know God and he
knows what it is to realize the presence of God.

Now on the one hand this is a high and difficult subject
and one about which people can often go astray; and yet on
the other hand we must be very careful not to stop short of
the fullness which the Scripture thus offers. There are two
types of knowledge of God which we must always hold.
There is, first of all, the knowledge of faith, the knowledge
that is common to most people who are at all religious. It
means a belief in God, a fulfilment of what the author of the
epistle to the Hebrews says in chapter eleven, verse 6, 'He
that cometh to God must believe that he is, and that he is a
rewarder of them that diligently seek him.' That is what I
call the knowledge of faith.

But something beyond that is offered to the Christian.
There is a kind of spiritual knowledge which is more direct
and more immediate, and which you will find often described in the psalms, under the Old Testament dispensation,
and also in the New Testament. You remember the knowledge of God that came to Moses when God put him in the
cleft of the rock so that Moses could have a glimpse of him as
be passed by. God revealed his glory to Moses and when he
came down from the Mount his face was shining with the
reflection of this divine glory. You find the apostle John
having a similar experience on the Isle of Patmos. It is just as
clear in the epistles; the apostle Paul knew what it was to be
taken up into the third heaven, and there to experience things
unseen and indescribable. He was a man, and yet he had that

amazing experience.

And it is not merely confined to the people of whom we read in the Bible. It is something which has been experienced on innumerable occasions by those of God's people who have realized the possibility of this, and have sought it as the most precious thing they could have in this life and in this world. One of the great Puritans, John Flavel, was taking a journey and suddenly, as he travelled along, God revealed himself to him. He did not have a vision, or see anything with the external eye, he just knew he was in the presence of the glory of God. He was so overwhelmed by it that he did not know how long he was there; he said that he 'utterly lost sight and sense of the world and all the concerns thereof'. He was, as it were, just enjoying the presence of the glory of God.

Those who have read the autobiography of Jonathan Edwards will know that he had a similar experience of just finding himself in the presence of the glory of God. Again, there was no vision but just this sense, this consciousness, of the reality and nearness, and the holiness and the majesty, of the glory of God.

You can read of the same thing in the the life of D. L. Moody, Moody was actually walking along Wall Street, New York, of all the streets in the world, when, suddenly, he had a similar experience. God, as it were, revealed and manifested himself to him in an immediate way; he had believed in him before, he had been used by him, he was a great Christian man, but here was something new, this consciousness of the immediate presence of God, the glory of God. It was such a marvellous thing that he turned into an hotel, and asked for a room for himself. He wanted to be alone and the glory became so tremendous that he asked God to withhold his hand lest it might crush him—the surpassing glory of it all.[1] I give these illustrations to impress the point that the possession of eternal life, which is life from God, leads to such a knowledge of God if we but realized it and cultivated it and developed it. And I do not hesitate to say that this is something which goes beyond the reaches of faith based upon knowledge. Genuine faith, established upon the full doctrine of the Bible, leads us to a knowledge of God which is more immediate and more direct, what the Puritans called a spiritual knowledge of God, over and above the knowledge of faith.

And that of course leads in turn to a fellowship with God. See this in 1 John 1. The old apostle realizes that he is coming to the end of his life, and as he writes to the young Christians in the churches, he tells them what he desires for them. It is that they might have fellowship with him, but, he says, not merely that they might have fellowship with him, because 'truly our fellowship is with the Father, and with his Son Jesus Christ'. I want you to know that, says John. I want you to know that in spite of things that may happen to you in this world, you can be enjoying active fellowship with God. You are meant to be walking with God now, and you are never meant to feel that you are alone. You are meant to know for certain that God and Christ are with you, and that your life is to be a walk and a pilgrimage in the presence of God the Father and God the Son, by the Holy Spirit which is in you. That fellowship is meant to be unbroken. Should you fall into sin, you will break the fellowship, and you will be so conscious of sin that you will be aware you have been left alone. But, says John, I want to assure you that if you realize what you have done, and if you confess and acknowledge it, and go back to God, the blood of Jesus Christ is still efficacious. Your sin will be wiped out, you will be renewed, and you will continue in this holy walk in life in the presence of God.

Christian people, that is the thing to which we are called, that is the kind of life we are meant to be living. That is eternal life—to be walking with God, to be sharing his life, and to be having fellowship with him; not feeling that God is a stranger far away from us, whom we try to find when we are in trouble, but realizing that we are always with him, always in his presence, conscious of his presence, and walking together in fellowship with him in the light. That is the Christian life, to be always with God, not just during our special times of prayer. Our whole life is to be lived in the conscious presence of God.

And that, in turn, leads to the next thing, which is that knowing him in this way we come especially to know his life. When the apostle Paul prayed for the Ephesian church, he prayed that they might know the love of Christ, the height, the depth, the length, the breadth of that love 'which passeth knowledge', that they might join together with all the saints in knowing this. You know, my friends, I feel increasingly that this is our greatest lack; it is the greatest need of the modern church and the modern Christian. What we do not realize—and it accounts for most of our errors and deficiencies—is the amazing love of God. Oh, if we but knew this love! If we but knew and understood something of the whole mystery of the incarnation and the atonement, this astounding love of his towards the world, in spite of its sin! But the man who has eternal life begins to know and to realize this. It becomes attractive to him, and that is why he is able to smile at cruel foes. He can know and say with the apostle Paul that nothing can separate him from the love of God.

So, then, the man who has eternal life is the man who knows God, the man who enters into an increasing awareness of the character and nature of God. Here again I would ask a question: as we look back across our lives and review them, can we say that we are coming to an increasingly greater knowledge of God? Do we feel that we understand the whole nature of God more than we did before? Is God becoming more and more real, and are we increasingly aware of his astounding, amazing love?

Let us now come on to the second big principle, which is that having eternal life means that we not only know God in that way, but we begin to become increasingly aware of our relationship to God. This is something that the apostles emphasized without ceasing. The man who has eternal life, says Paul, is the man who has the spirit of adoption, who now really knows God as his Father, and I suppose it is in a sense the distinguishing feature of Christianity. The Jews of old believed in God in a general sense, in God as Creator, in God as the Maker of the world, but, surely, the special thing that our Lord introduced was this sure and certain knowledge and assurance of God as Father. 'Ye have received,' says Paul, 'the spirit of adoption, whereby we cry, Abba Father' (Rom 8:15). Now that is inevitable, of course, from äll we have been saying; it is the inevitable outcome of our knowledge of God. We begin to realize the truth about ourselves in our relationship to God, and I know of nothing which will enable us to know more certainly whether or not we have received this gift of eternal life than our answer to a simple question: when we think of God and when we come into his presence, what is our thought, what is our idea of God? Do we realize and know for certain that he is our Father? When we say, 'Our Father which art in heaven' do we really mean that?

Our Lord described this in the Sermon on the Mount. He was anticipating there what was to be true of the Christian and he says, You should not worry about food and clothing, 'for your heavenly Father knoweth that ye have need of all these things' (Mt 6:32). We are coming to our Father, and as we come to him we should realize that he is our Father. Indeed, we should not only believe that, we should have a consciousness of it, the spirit of adoption which makes us cry, Abba Father—this intimate relationship. The Christian begins to realize that God is indeed his Father, that the hairs of his head are all numbered, and that his relationship to God is not something mechanical, it is experiential. That, of course, leads to a sense of dependence upon God, and the consciousness that, as time passes, we are in his hands. And that, further, means that we begin to look to him for strength, and for power, and for everything.

Oh, what fools we are! I make no apology for using such a phrase. How foolish we are as Christian people in failing to realize that in this relationship to God our every need can be supplied and our every want satisfied. The life that was lived by the Lord Jesus Christ here on earth, he himself tells us repeatedly, was a life that was lived in constant dependence upon his Father. He says, 'The words that I speak unto you I speak not of myself: but the Father that dwelleth in me, he doeth the works' (Jn 14:10). But it is only as we realize this that we begin to understand why our Lord ever prayed. So many people cannot understand why the Son of God prayed while he was here on earth. The answer is that his life as a man was dependent upon God. He looked to God for the works he was to do and received power to perform them by receiving the Holy Spirit. He was constantly being filled with the Holy Spirit that was given to him without measure, and it was in this strength and power that he offered up himself. It was through the Spirit that he offered himself up to God, and he was 'declared to be the Son of God with power, according to the spirit of holiness, by the resurrection from the dead' (Rom 1:4).

This is surely one of the most staggering things that man can ever learn in this world, but it is an essential part of knowing God. And thus you find, as you read the lives of the saints throughout the ages, that they have always been people who have spent much of their time in prayer. They realized that they were supposed to live this life as Christ lived it in dependence upon God, so they did not rely upon their own strength and ability. They sought his mind and will, they sought the fullness of the Spirit, they sought the power which God alone could give and they drew from God and lived their life of victory and triumph.

But I want to emphasize another suggestive aspect of this great life, which is that the man who has eternal life not only knows God and his relationship to him, he delights in God, and his supreme desire is to know God better. Here again I take you back to the psalms. Do you remember what David felt like when he came again to the house of God? He tells us, 'As the hart panteth after the water brooks so . . . my soul thirsteth for God, for the living God' (Ps 42:1–2). Now that inevitably happens if we possess eternal life; like always attracts like. The characteristic of love is that it desires to be in the presence of the object of its love, and the receiving of eternal life leads to that attitude with respect to God. And thus you find, as you read your Scriptures about these holy men of God and as you read the lives of all the saints, that their greatest desire was to know God better. They were always seeking his presence, and an ever greater realization of it. It was this that led them to examine themselves every day and to discover how they lived. It was this which made that saintly man John Fletcher ask himself a series of questions when he went to bed every night. These questions were all destined to establish this point: had he been walking with God as he should have been? Had this walk been neglected in his life? Had there been any break in the fellowship? Had sin come in and spoilt and tarnished it? This is something that is universally true of all the saints, whatever the century, whatever the nation to which they belong; they have set before them, above everything else, a realization of the presence of God, and they have done so because they have delighted in him. To spend time in reading the Bible and in meditation is no burden to those who have eternal life. They delight in it, it is their greatest joy, because knowing God as they know him, they enjoy him. The first question of the shorter Catechism is: 'What is the chief end of man?' The answer is, 'The chief end of man is to glorify God and to enjoy him for ever.' And you cannot read the Bible honestly without seeing that those who are described in the Old Testament knew and enjoyed God and enjoyed living their life with him. Our Lord's chief delight was to be talking to

his Father, to be communing with him. He enjoyed God and
we are meant to enjoy God. Oh, God should not be a task-
master to the man who has eternal life, to the man who is a
true Christian! God should be the supreme object of his joy
and his delight and of his pleasure.

My friends, if we but knew God in his holy, loving,
character, if we but knew his love, we would want to spend
our whole life in his presence and with him. That is the thing
to which these men were looking forward. 'That I may
know him,' says Paul; he is forgetting the things that are
behind and he is looking forward to this unmixed enjoyment
of God in heaven. That is the reality of heaven, to be basking
in the love and glory of God. The man who receives eternal
life begins to awaken to these things. I do not want to dis-
courage anybody. I am describing this life in its fullness, but
I am obviously suggesting, as I do so, that if we are utter
strangers to this and know nothing about it, even in the most
elementary form, then it is time we asked ourselves whether
we have received eternal life. Am I a Christian at all? Do I
know anything about these things? Have I ever had a passing
second in my life in which I have known something of God
and realized his presence and known something of his
astounding love? The man who has this life is the man who
loves God. You see, God does not stop at asking us to
believe in him. 'The first and great commandment,' says our
Lord, is, 'Thou shalt love the Lord thy God. . .' Faith is
insufficient, we are meant to go on to love God and to love
him with the whole of our being.

But obviously I must come to the next principle, which is
that the man who has eternal life loves to do the will of God.
That is the logical sequence. The man who loves is the man
who is anxious to please the object of his love. There is no
better test of love than that, and unless you desire to please
someone whom you claim to love, then I assure you, you do
not love that person. Love always wants to be pleasing and
to give itself, and anyone who loves God wants to do the

will of God. If you look at Christ, you see that the whole of his life, his one object, was to do the will of his Father. He did not care what it was; even in the Garden of Gethsemane when he faced the one thing he did not want, even there he said, 'Nevertheless not my will, but thine, be done' (Lk 22:42). He says, I do not want to drink this cup, but if it is doing thy will, I will do even that—that is love at its maximum and its best, and it is true of all who have his life. The chief end of the true Christian is the glory of God, therefore he spends his time in seeking to know the will of God and in doing it. He strives to do it and he loves to do it. He is controlled by this one idea. Having learnt what God has done for him and what God is to him, having realized something of this love of God, he says, 'Love so amazing, so divine, demands my soul, my life, my all.' And man, therefore, who has eternal life, has this as the supreme object and desire of his life, to do the will of God.

And this brings me to my last word. The ultimate manifestation of the possession of eternal life is that it produces certain results in our lives. Fortunately for us they have all been set out in a very brief compass by the apostle Paul in Galatians 5, verses 22 and 23, where he talks of the fruit of the Spirit. A man once said a very profound thing when he described these verses as 'The shortest biography of Christ that has ever been written.' He was absolutely right. That is the perfect description of the life of the Lord Jesus Christ; those were its characteristics—'love, joy, peace, longsuffering, gentleness, goodness, faith [or faithfulness], meekness, temperance', and anyone who has received this gift of eternal life from him is one who in turn begins to manifest that sort of life; that is the kind of person he becomes. 'The kingdom of God,' says Paul to the Romans, 'is not meat and drink; but righteousness, and peace, and joy in the Holy Ghost' (Rom 14:17). 'The carnal mind is enmity against God' (Rom 8:7); 'to be carnally minded is death; but to be spiritually minded is life and peace' (Rom 8:6). So that as we examine ourselves at this moment, we must again ask ourselves this vital question: can Christ fulfill in me the object of his coming and dying? He says he has done it all to give eternal life. Have I received eternal life? And a very good way of testing it is to ask further: is the fruit of the Spirit manifesting itself in me? Because Christ is the eternal life and the Spirit produces its fruit in us.

Do you know this life of God in your own life? Have you this joy in the Holy Ghost, something that makes you independent of circumstances? Do you know a great peace in your heart, peace within, peace with other people, something that, whatever happens, leaves you unruffled. Are you longsuffering? He was longsuffering when he suffered the contradiction of sinners against himself. Are we gentle; are we good; are we patient with people or do we lose our tempers with them? Are we constantly manifesting our irritability and touchiness, or do we manifest longsuffering, gentleness and goodness, faithfulness, meekness, humility and temperance—or self-control? Is there a discipline in our lives? There is a control and balance in living the life of Christ. See these things and remember that he offered them to us. And I put these questions not only that we may know these things here and now, but that we may *enjoy* them. We can receive the gift of eternal life in this life and in this world, but if we die without receiving it, we cannot possibly enjoy the life of God in eternity. This is but a preparation, it is a foretaste. We are not given the full possession of the great estate, but we are given the seal, the earnest, the title deeds, so that I know I am going to get it all, because of what I receive now. And if I have not received the title deeds and the earnest of the inheritance here, it just means that I will never receive the full inheritance there.

Have you received eternal life, my friends? The most momentous challenge you have ever faced is the Lord Jesus Christ who died on the cross and who rose again to give you this gift. Do you find something of this life in you? If you do, well pledge yourself from this moment to live for it, to receive more of it, that it may grow and develop. But if you feel you have never received this life, hasten away quietly somewhere into the presence of God and tell him you see clearly that you have never had it; acknowledge and confess your sin to him, and give up relying upon yourself and your own goodness.

This is the test of a Christian, not to be better than anybody else, not to be a church member, not simply to hold certain views, nor to pride yourself in some strict morality. No, this is the test of Christianity and nothing less, and if you realize that you do not have it, confess it to God, confess all your self-righteousness, acknowledge it all. Cast yourself upon God's offer of salvation freely in Christ who has died for you, and ask him to give you this gift of eternal life, this gift of life divine which is life indeed. And once you have it, you will begin to manifest these things and you will begin to live for God and his glory and to enjoy him. Religion will no longer be a task, it will be your chiefest delight. I end as I began, and ask you to pray:

> Breathe on me, Breath of God,
> Fill me with life anew,
> That I may love what Thou dost love,
> And do what Thou would'st do.

---

[1] For a fuller treatment of these experiences, readers might be interested to read M. Lloyd-Jones, *Joy Unspeakable* (Kingsway, 1984).

13

Safe in His Eternal Kingdom

John 17:1–5

Perhaps it is as well, at this point, to remind ourselves of the fact that when our blessed Lord and Saviour offered this prayer to his Father, he did so audibly. It was a prayer addressed to God, but it was meant to be overheard by the disciples. And the whole character of the prayer, not only in this first section, which we have been considering, but the entire prayer as recorded in the whole chapter, drives us to the same conclusion—that our Lord had one great object in thus praying this prayer audibly, and that was that these disciples and followers of his might know for certain the security of their position. The whole tenor of the prayer is that our Lord is handing over these disciples to God the Father, and praying to him to look after them, as it were, and he does so audibly in order that they might know that. But in so doing, he enters into certain details, and it is as we look at these details, as we have been doing, that we really grasp all the great and high doctrine, and come to the conclusion that our position is safe and secure.

In other words, we have been engaged in an analysis of these verses, in order that we all might really find ourselves experiencing what Augustus Toplady expresses in his well-known hymn, that position in which a man is confident and assured, certain that nothing can ever separate him from the love of God:

> Things future, nor things that are now,
> Nor all things below or above,
> Can make Him His purpose forego,
> Or sever my soul from His love.

That is the great doctrine that is announced here in these verses—the security of the believer. Our Lord was coming to the end of his earthly life. He was leaving the world and going back to God to share that eternal glory in all its fullness, and our Lord's great concern was that these followers of his—and through them all who would believe because of their preaching and all Christians in all ages everywhere—should know for certain the security of their position. And we find it, as a result, one of the greatest themes in all the New Testament epistles. In a sense, that is why every one of these epistles was written, in order that all Christians might *know*, and the writers exhort them to live a certain type of life because of this. Christians are not exhorted to do certain things in order that they ultimately might arrive in heaven. Rather, they are told to live this kind of life because they are destined for it, and it is because of this that sin is so unthinkable, and so incompatible.

John summarizes that in his first epistle when he says, 'Every man that hath this hope in him purifieth himself' (1 Jn 3:3), so the great thing is to know that we have this hope. You find it again, for example, in Hebrews 6, where the author exhorts the Hebrew Christians to continue to give diligence to good works, 'to the full assurance of hope unto the end' (verse 11)—it is the same thought. He wants them to know that they have an anchor within the veil, 'Whither,' he says, 'the forerunner is for us entered' (verse 20). That is the way to live the Christian life. The Christian was never meant to go through this world haltingly and uncertainly, wondering whether he is a Christian, hoping that sometime or other before death something may suddenly happen to

him. No, he should start in this position and he should walk
steadfastly and assuredly in the diretion of his eternal hope.
That, I say, is the purpose of this great prayer and it comes
out especially in the great and high doctrine we have looked
at together in these first five verses. Indeed, it has been our
object and endeavour, as we have been considering them, to
bring out that aspect of the truth, in order that we all might
enjoy 'the full assurance of hope right unto the end'.

Now we have been doing it in a detailed manner, and
what I want to do here is to try to sum it all up and to take
one of those synoptic views of the whole, so that we may see
ourselves as we are in God's great plan and purpose. We have
outlined that as it is taught here and we have seen certain
things about it. We have seen that it is not something contingent or fortuitous, it is something that has been planned, and
the names of God's people have been written in the Lamb's
book of life from before the foundation of the world. That is
the starting point and we have looked at it as it is unfolded
and as it has been enacted and brought to pass in this world.
In other words, our salvation is dependent upon God's eternal purpose, carried out in history, so that we are not saved
by ideas or by theories, but by certain things that have been
done and enacted once and for ever. Our salvation must
always be thought of in those terms and categories. It belongs to history and it is as definitely historical as the fact that
Julius Caesar invaded Britain in 55 BC. It is all dependent on
certain events, things that have actually taken place. So, having gone into these things in detail, I want now to gather up
the grounds for our belief in the security of the Christian
believer, and to put it in the form of a number of principles.

First, we are told that the Christian is one who has been
chosen by God and has been given by God to his Son, our
Lord and Saviour Jesus Christ: 'As thou hast given him
power over all flesh, that he should give eternal life to as
many as thou hast given him.' Now that is a vital statement.
I wonder whether you have ever noticed that our Lord

repeats it seven times in this one chapter. I do not want you to become interested merely statistically—that is not the point—but I do want you to see the importance of this statement. There it is in the second verse: 'that he should give eternal life to as many as thou hast given him'. Then in verse 6, he says, 'I have manifested thy name unto the men which thou gavest me out of the world', and again 'thine they were, and thou gavest them me'—so he says it twice in that sixth verse. Then we find it again in the ninth verse: 'I pray for them'—notice this—'I pray not for the world, but for them which thou hast given me; for they are thine.' He does not pray for the world, he prays only for those who belong to God and whom God has given to him—there is the great division. Then we find it in verse 11: 'And now,' he says, 'I am no more in the world, but these are in the world, and I come to thee. Holy Father, keep through thine own name those whom thou hast given me, that they may be one, as we are.' It is the same reference. And again in the next verse: 'While I was with them in the world, I kept them in thy name: those that thou gavest me I have kept, and none of them is lost, but the son of perdition.' And finally we are given it for the last time in verse 24: 'Father, I will that they also, whom thou hast given me, be with me where I am; that they may behold my glory, which thou hast given me: for thou lovedst me before the foundation of the world.'

Now the plain teaching of these scriptures is obviously that God the Father has given a certain people to God the Son, and the Son has come into this world specifically to give eternal life to those people and to nobody else.

'Ah,' you say, 'but I do not understand that sort of doctrine!'

But I am simply explaining to you the statement of the Scriptures. If there is any other conceivable explanation of these statements I shall be interested to hear what it is. This is not my theory, or that of any other man. Our Lord says it seven times in this one chapter, and it is a statement you find repeatedly running through the Scriptures, namely that God his Father has given him, as it were, a mass of people, that he should give eternal life 'to as many as thou hast given me'. So that the business of the Son is to give eternal life to each one of those people. That is what our Lord himself says in this great high priestly prayer under the very shadow of the cross.

But when I say something like this, people immediately begin to ask questions. They say, 'I do not understand the love of God that can do this for some and not for others.'

My dear friends, I do not understand it, neither does anybody else understand it. Our business is to come to Scripture and to believe it. I do not pretend to understand the eternal mind of God and how it works. I am not meant to do that. This is the trouble with the philosophers. They say that they do not understand how God can to this or that, they want to explain the mind of the almighty God with their pigmy minds and it cannot be done. And that is why the philosophers find it so difficult to become Christians. All I know is that the blessed Son of God, standing in this world, says, 'I pray not for the world'; he prays only for those whom God has given him. He does not even say that he has chosen them, he says that God the Father has chosen them and given him these people. And as I understand this doctrine, it is that when the Son came from heaven, he came with a great commission from the Father. It was that he should do certain things in this world in order that he could give eternal life to those people whom God had set apart unto himself and whom he had given to the Son as his inheritance.

If you trace that doctrine through the Scriptures, you will find it in the Old Testament quite as plainly as in the New; you will find it everywhere. Your salvation and mine was something that was known to God, and our names written in the Lamb's book of life, before the creation of the world. You do not understand it, neither do I, but, thank God, we are not saved by our understanding, but by our acceptance of

the truth. Indeed, it is quite unscriptural for men and women
to put their intellectual difficulties before the plain statement
of Scripture, and I think we need to reconsider this matter. It
is not a bit surprising that we find it difficult to equate certain
scriptural statements with our conception of the love of God.
But the apostle Paul in his letter to the Corinthians, says that
'It pleased God by the foolishness of preaching to save them
that believe' (1 Cor 1:21), but the wise, those people who
trust to their own understanding are confused—'to the
Greeks foolishness'.

My dear friends, the way to start considering these matters
is just to remind yourself of what you are. Measure your
mind, which you have set up as the ultimate court of appeal
and authority, how big is it? What do we really understand
with our minds? Do we understand ourselves, do we understand life, do we understand the whole mystery and marvel
of creation? Do we understand 'the meanest flower that
blows', electricity, or something as small as an atom? Of
course we do not! And yet we put up our little minds against
the mind of God. Our minds are too small, their scope is too
limited. But that is not the whole truth about us. Not only
are our faculties limited to start with, we are, furthermore,
sinful creatures. We see nothing straight and everything is
influenced by that fact. Our mind is naturally at enmity with
God and all our understanding is defective, tarnished and
soiled by sin.

That is why the Christian position is that henceforth I
cease to put anything in terms of 'my mind and my understanding'. And I come as a little child to the Bible, realizing
that it will not be open to me except my mind be enlightened
by the Holy Spirit—so I do not trust to my mind. Faith
means that we voluntarily and deliberately open ourselves up
to the revelation of the Bible and that when we do not
understand things we say, 'I do not understand, but I am
content not to understand. I believe the word of God and I
rest myself and my whole position entirely upon it.' That is

the faith position. The moment that you begin to bring in your mind and natural arguments and say that you cannot see or understand something, you are turning from the revelation and are reverting back to the sinful position of putting your mind up as the supreme court of appeal. In Romans 8 we are told that 'whom he did foreknow, he also did predestinate to be conformed to the image of his Son . . . and whom he called, them he also justified: and whom he justified, them he also glorified' (verses 29–30). He has done it; the Christian is already glorified as he is justified in the sight of God, though still on earth. He may be 'accounted as sheep for the slaughter' (verse 36), but he is glorified. God does not do things in a piecemeal manner, he does everything as a whole, and he knows his people. 'The foundation of God standeth sure, having this seal. The Lord knoweth them that are his' (2 Tim 2:19). God has known his people from the very beginning, and he has separated them unto himself. Paul prays for the Ephesians that the eyes of their understanding may be enlightened, that they may know 'what is the hope of his calling and what the riches of the glory of his inheritance in the saints' (1:18). It is the same doctrine; we find it everywhere in the Bible.

So, this is the first basis and ground of our security and our assurance. My assurance rests upon the fact that, if I am a Christian at all, I am a Christian because God has chosen me unto salvation and separated me; he has taken me out of it all, and has given me to his Son that the Son might give me eternal life. What a blessed basis on which to live! What an astounding fact! Oh, the unutterable folly of men and women who try by philosophy to understand the inscrutable, the eternal, and reject such a doctrine! Some people believe that you can receive eternal life from the blessed Son of God and then lose it, then regain it, and then lose it again, and go on thus uncertainly in this world until you come to die. My friends, it is an insult to God! It is an insult to God's glorious plan of redemption, it is an insult to God's eternal way of doing things—'that he should give eternal life to as many as thou hast given him'. What a conception, that God has given me to Christ, that Christ might save me and might give me eternal life.

That is the first ground, but let us come to another. The second basis of security and assurance, according to our Lord, is that every hindrance and obstacle to our receiving this gift of eternal life has been removed by the blessed work of the Lord himself. 'I have glorified thee on the earth: I have finished the work which thou gavest me to do.' Many things have had to be done before I could receive the gift of eternal life. As a natural man I wondered how I could get it. Now we have already considered what it is. You remember that eternal life really means that we are sharers of the life of God and are in communion with him. Is it not obvious, therefore, that a great many things have to happen before we can come into that condition? So, thank God, my second ground for assurance is that it has all been done. There is nothing that has been left undone. He has dealt with the problem of my guilt, by removing it. He has reconciled me to God, the law of God has been satisfied—'Who shall lay any thing to the charge of God's elect?' (Rom 8:33). I can ask, and without any qualification: 'Is there anybody anywhere who can bring any charge against me as a child of God?' There is none, for, 'It is God that justifieth' (Rom 8:33). He himself has done it for, 'It is Christ that died, yea rather, that is risen again, who is even at the right hand of God' (verse 34).

Christian people, *this* is the position we are meant to occupy. Let me quote another hymn of Augustus Toplady:

> The terrors of law and of God
> With me can have nothing to do.
> My Saviour's obedience and blood,
> Hide all my transgressions from view.

That is not boasting for I am not relying upon myself, but upon him—'My Saviour's obedience and blood, hide all my transgressions from view', and unless you can say that, there is something defective about your faith. Far from being boastful, that is the thing that humbles a man, the thing that makes him strive after holiness, because it is true. Or take again that line.

> Of covenant mercy I sing.

Now that is what our Lord is saying here. He tells his Father that all which was necessary has been done, the guilt removed, the law satisfied, the Father reconciled, the new nature given, the Holy Spirit given, and the work going on until ultimately this child of God will find himself faultless and blameless without spot or blemish, perfect in the presence of God. Our security is that the work has been done, every hindrance, every obstacle, every barrier has been removed, because Christ has done it all, He said, 'I go to prepare a place for you' (Jn 14:2), and he has done what he promised, so that the ultimate outcome is, as Toplady says—

> More happy but not more secure,
> The glorified spirits in heaven.

What a statement to make! According to Augustus Toplady, on the basis of these things, the glorified spirits in heaven are not more secure than we are here on earth, because our security is in Christ. Of course, they are happier than we are, they are in a land where there is no sin, no shame, no sorrow, no sighing; more happy—yes—but they are not more secure.

And I will tell you why this is so. To be a Christian, you see, does not just mean that I believe on the Lord Jesus Christ and have my sins forgiven. It also means that I am in Christ, I am in him and he is in me. I am a part of him; I have died with him; I have risen with him. He is my life and I am in him. So, being in him, I am as secure as those who are with him in heaven, and it is because he has dealt with every barrier and hindrance and obstacle to our receiving this blessed life.

Then the third ground and basis of my security and assurance is the very character and nature of the life itself. I need not dilate on this, because we have already spent some time in considering it. But to make this statement complete, I must just refer to it in passing. You remember that the nature of the life is that we really do become 'partakers of the divine nature', that we are born of God, that we are his children and that we are sharers in the life of God himself. Now I argue that because of that, it is something which cannot come and go. It cannot change. It is something which is stable and everlasting. It is, indeed, *eternal* life, and we saw as we analysed it that 'eternal' implies duration. We are all destined either for eternal life or for a life of condemnation and destruction, and they both go on for ever. Eternal life is the life of God, and because of that, it is everlasting, so it is eternal life in that sense.

I find it quite extraordinary that anybody calling himself a Christian can believe that he can receive this gift of the life of God, and then, because of sin, lose it and then accept it again and then lose it once more. You cannot go on being born and dying! No, if you receive the life of God, then God himself gives you this gift through his Son, and the very quality, the nature and character of the life means that it is imperishable. Our Lord has already said this in the gospel of John, 'Neither shall any man pluck them out of my hand' (Jn 10:28)—it is impossible. Or again, the apostle Paul says, 'Neither death, nor life, nor angels, nor principalities, nor powers, nor things present, nor things to come, nor height, nor depth, nor any other creature, shall be able to separate us from the love of God, which is in Christ Jesus our Lord' (Rom 8:38– 39). Furthermore, this is especially true because he himself has given us this life. So we are in this new relationship, we belong to the family of God, we are separated out of the world, we are separated unto God, we are a part of his plan and purpose, and we belong to him. That is why Paul can say with such confidence that 'the sufferings of this present time are not worthy to be compared with the glory which shall be revealed in us' (Rom 8:18). We are saved by hope, hope which is sure and certain, because it is based upon the character, indeed upon the life, of God himself. Therefore, if we know that we have eternal life, it should encourage us, and strengthen us. It should enable us to know that because God has given us that gift, it is indeed, as God himself has said, an *eternal* life.

'Well, then,' says someone, 'because I am saved, it means that I can blaspheme and do anything I like.' But the man who knows that he has eternal life, never reasons like that— 'Every man that hath his hope in him purifieth himself, even as he is pure' (1 Jn 3:3). The man who knows that he has eternal life, and that he is going on to face God in heaven, is the man above everybody else who is going to be striving after holiness. That has always been the case, it is the argument of the Scriptures, and that is how God's people have argued throughout the centuries. Did you know that foreign mission work was started originally by people who believed things like this? The greatest motive of the missionary enterprise has always been that they have known that God is the means as well as the end. They have believed that God has called them to propagate the gospel, and because of that they have sacrificed everything, even their lives, and gone and preached. The man who is most ready to sacrifice his life for the gospel is the man who knows that even death cannot separate him from the love of God and that he has the life of God in him. This is why the men who believe these truths have always been the greatest workers in the kingdom of God. It has been their certain knowledge that they are the children of God and possessors of eternal life.

My next basis is one of the most precious of all. We must work out the argument based upon the fact that our Lord has suffered so much and so many things, in order that all this might be possible for us. This is his statement, 'I have glorified thee on the earth: I have finished the work which thou gavest me to do.' He was referring to his coming from heaven, to the fact that he had laid aside the signs of his glory. He did not clutch at his power or exhalt it. Though he was in equality with God, he humbled himself and decided to live as man. He relied entirely upon God and the gift of the Holy Spirit which he received. He humbled himself. He endured the contradiction of sinners, and he sweated blood in the Garden of Gethsemane. He staggered beneath the weight of the cruel cross, the nails were hammered into his hands and feet, he suffered intolerable thirst, and he died. He has done all that, so then—this is the argument—'If, when we were enemies, we were reconciled to God by the death of his Son, much more, being reconciled, shall we be saved by his life' (Rom 5:10); 'He that spared not his own Son, but delivered him up for us all, how shall he not with him also freely give us all things?' (Rom 8:32).

This logic is quite inevitable and I work it out like this: Christ has borne and suffered all that for me in order that he might give me the gift of eternal life. So, in the light of that, is it still feasible to believe that he should do all that for me and my salvation and then suddenly leave me and let me perish? It is impossible! 'If, when we were enemies, we were reconciled to God by the death of his Son, much more, being reconciled, shall we be saved'—and saved to the very end—'by his life' (Rom 5:10). What a wonderful powerful argument this is! I believe that is why he prayed aloud in the presence of these men, 'I have glorified thee on the earth: I have finished the work which thou gavest me to do.' I have done all this for them, and if I have done all this for them, I will never leave them to perish or sink now.

We must understand that argument and employ it. The Son of God has done the greatest thing for us and he will never fail us. If he suffered even to the cross, there, glorified in heaven, 'He ever liveth to make intercession for them' (Heb 7:25). This is the logic, according to the author of the epistle to the Hebrews. 'He saves to the uttermost. . .' (verse

25), to the very end. He will never fail, for his blood, his cross, is a guarantee of that. If he had come to do the work while here on earth, how much more will he do it now in heaven, in his glorified state. So as we use that argument we find it a great and grand basis of security and assurance.

But the last basis on which I stand, is the one which he puts in these words: 'As thou hast given him power over all flesh, that he should give eternal life to as many as thou hast given him.' It is a literal statement of fact. God the Father has given to the Son, the Lord Jesus Christ, power over all flesh, over everything—there is nothing that is not placed under him. That is Scripture again. You realize what that means. The universe, the cosmos, every star in its orbit, the sun and moon, every power, every atom with its magnetic force and power, all are under his power. Everything in nature and creation, man and all his powers, his devices, his machinations, everything that he is capable of doing, it is all under the power of God, under the power of Christ.

It goes even beyond that. The future is in his hands. There is a picture in Revelation of the book that was sealed up, and we are told that no one was found who was big enough or strong enough to open the book of the course of history, until suddenly there appeared the Lion of Judah. He prevailed because he was strong enough and mighty enough to open the book. All this simply means that the whole of future history is in the hands of the Lord Jesus Christ. You may be worried about the international situation, you need not be, nor about any earthly force or power, because the whole of history is in his hands. Of course, we do not understand it all. He permits many things that we do not understand, but the fact that he permits it means that it is still in his power. There is nothing out of hand.

I want to go one step further and say that the devil is under his power. The devil is under the control of Christ, because he has absolute power and even the devil is subject to it. Christ has conquered, and what the devil does is under the sufferance of God, for God's inscrutable reason and purpose. We are so clever with our philosophies that we say, 'Now why did God do that? Why didn't he decide to make us perfect? Why is Satan allowed to do this?' And we go on asking our questions. But the faith position is that you and I just humble ourselves as little children, and bow to the fact that God has so ordered and ordained it. He has determined the times, but there is a very definite limit to the time. God knows the day on which the Lord Jesus Christ will come back into this world. Men, and nations, and powers, and all that is opposed to God, will be taken by him and cast into the lake of perdition, and he will give the final proof that all flesh has been subjected to him and to his almighty power.

But the argument here is that all power has been given to him over all flesh in order that he might give eternal life. So Christ has done all that I have described in order to give to me the gift of eternal life. In this life and world the flesh is within me, and it drags me down. There are lusts and passions and desires in me. There is no such thing as a perfect human being in this world, even though he may be a Christian. Things are here trying to drag me down and to rob me of eternal life. Against me are the world and the devil, who even tempted the blessed Son of God. How can I stand against all this? There is only one way: he is able to control it all. The guarantee that you and I can arrive in heaven and in glory is that he does control it all and that we are saved in spite of the world and the flesh and the devil. This is because the 'power that worketh in us' is the power of God, the power that brought Christ from the dead, and it enables us to go through and beyond it all.

Paul puts it in as extreme a form as this. There are, he says, certain preachers who are building upon a foundation of wood and hay and stubble. And at the end, when the testing comes, all their works will be burnt and destroyed, so that there will be nothing left. It will all be burnt up because it was so shoddy and useless. Yet, he says, they themselves will be saved 'so as by fire' (1 Cor 3:12–15). And what has saved them? It is this power of the Lord over all flesh. He suffers us to be tried and tempted, but he will never suffer us to be lost. No man, nothing, can pluck us out of his hand. He exercises the power, and he will continue to do so, so that neither man, nor history, nor the devil, nor hell, nor anything at all can ever separate us from him. So in the words of the hymn we can say—

> From Him who loves me now so well
> What power my soul can sever?
> Shall life or death, shall earth or hell?
> No, I am His for ever.
>
> *James Grindlay Small*

My dear friend, if you are relying upon your love for him or upon your grasp or hold of him, I am sorry for you. I pity you, because my only reliance is upon him. The gift he gives us is eternal life—it is himself. So the end and the consummation of all this is that we must trust, and trust alone, to the faithfulness of Christ. He has done everything for you and he will hold you and save you to the end, and will present you faultless before the presence of God's glory with exceeding joy. Oh, how we should thank him that he offered this prayer audibly, that we might know where we stand, and know that we are surrounded by his love, and saved eternally, safe in his eternal kingdom.